C000274165

Under The Asylum Tree

SURVIVORS' POETRY

ILLUSTRATED ANTHOLOGY

Under The Asylum Tree

SURVIVORS' POETRY

ILLUSTRATED ANTHOLOGY

SURVIVORS' PRESS 1995

For all survivors – wherever they may be.

Publication Data

Published in 1995
by

Survivors' Press
Diorama Arts Centre
34 Osnaburgh Street
London NW1 3ND

(We regret that we cannot accept unsolicited MSS.)

All rights reserved on behalf of each artist
and writer represented in this book.

Copyright in the poems remains with the author © 1995
Copyright in the illustrations remains with the artist © 1995
The collection copyright remains with Survivors' Press © 1995

No part of this publication may be reproduced, stored in a retrieval
system, or transmitted in any form, or by any means, electronic,
mechanical, photocopying, recording or otherwise, without prior
permission of the respective author or artist.*(See Page 201.)*

British Library Cataloguing-in-Publication Data
A catalogue record for this book
is available from the British Library
ISBN 1 874595 01 1 (paperback)

Editorial Acknowledgements
Edited by Jenny Ford, Colin Hambrook & Hilary Porter
for SURVIVORS' POETRY
Front cover illustration by Jan Marshall
Design by Colin Hambrook & David Russell
Co-ordinator – Joe Bidder

Typeset using Palatino 10pt
by David Russell
8 McGregor Road, London W11 1DE

Printed in Great Britain
by Antony Rowe, Chippenham, Wiltshire

FOREWORD

This publication is the second collection published by Survivors' Press. Our first anthology *from dark to light* was short-listed for the MIND Book of the Year Award and the Arts Council/Raymond Williams Community Publishing Prize. Selling out of two editions, it has been instrumental in inspiring many survivor poets throughout the U.K. and elsewhere.

This new and larger collection features the work of 94 survivor poets, artists and kindred spirits. More than 1000 poems and illustrations were submitted from all regions of the U.K. and from abroad, covering a wide range of subject matter and style.

Established since 1991, SURVIVORS' POETRY is managed by mental health system survivors. Now a registered charity, it operates nationally, providing a quality literature resource through a programme of workshops, readings, performances, outreach, networking and training.

Funded by the Arts Council of England and the London Arts Board it organises more than 120 events per year. Workshops and performances are brought into diverse communities: schools, hospitals, youth projects, day centres, community centres, universities, poetry venues, disability arts projects, bookshops, literature and arts festivals. Collaborative projects are an important feature: joint events are organised with well-known community groups, regional arts groups, local government, poetry & festivals organisations. We are grateful for support from many individuals and organisations, some of whom are listed in this publication.

An extensive outreach activity has led to the formation of regional survivor poetry groups in Andover, Exeter, Leeds, Liverpool, Manchester, Swindon & Wolverhampton. A second UK Tour is planned for 1995 and we hope that additional regional groups will be founded by local survivor poets.

More than 150 poets and musicians have been employed from diverse cultures. Featuring survivor, disabled and non-survivor established poets & artists, performances usually include floor spots for new and aspiring poets – many of whom have subsequently obtained featured performances and paid work at other established poetry and performance venues.

In the past four years, national newspaper articles, radio and television programmes have featured SURVIVORS' POETRY and individual poets. The media are simultaneously congratulatory and puzzled by the success of this movement. Survivors of the mental health system have a unique voice and experience to communicate to the world. Our creativity, coupled with the consistent organisational skills to operate an extensive national programme of work, have effectively countered a negative stereotypical image with a positive example of self-empowerment.

SURVIVORS' POETRY opposes, by artistic achievement & social practices, the negative images and reporting prevalent today in national & local media and society at large.

INTRODUCTION – little black bears

You must **verbalise!**

That was the greeting I received from the hospital psychiatrist when I proffered my case history in the form of a neatly written dossier. Having spent, as it seemed, an agonized eternity ripping hardened scar tissue off long buried traumas, I was in no mood to repeat the experience.

Result! Weeks of secure, locked wards and stubborn drug-soaked silence whilst a stupid and sadistic (as I saw him) shrink tried to break down the verbal barriers. He failed miserably and I was released into the mainstream of the hospital.

In occupational therapy, the lady in charge of creative writing and poetry reading noticed faint flickers of interest. Leading me to a bright cheerful room overlooking the grounds, she put me in front of a typewriter and **gently** asked me to try and write something, anything, **if and when I felt like it.**

I had never used a typewriter and stared at it fearfully. Eventually I tapped a key. A little black bear appeared on the vast white plain. I tapped again. Another little bear! It must have been the mating season because soon hundreds of little black bears bounced all over the page.

My first poem! Dredged from the deepest pit it squatted there, dripping slime and misery all over the page. But it was out. At last I'd found a way to exorcise the "mind monsters".

The articles about SURVIVORS' POETRY in the *The Guardian* and *New Women* in 1992 have made me very happy. At last, the world had become aware of the value of creativity as an alternative to conventional, mind mugging, medication.

When the lady put me in front of that typewriter she gave me a gift beyond price. In the two years since writing that first poem my life has changed completely. I discovered that writing is the dialysis of my depression and that I can function reasonably well with regular treatment.

My sanity depends on writing. The chemical **mind clamp** which replaced the canvas **body curb** had muzzled me into non-productive frustration; and therefore actually caused depression. Writing puts sense and order in my life.

I learned to type, to use a word processor and dictaphone. I joined a writing group. I wrote endless poems and even had a few published. I have written and am editing a full length novel, a thriller. I shall try to get published but if I were never to have anything published I would still write.

Before all this, at fifty years of age, I drove a truck!

But now I have found my place and my tribe.

George MacDonald
County Wexford
Ireland

CONTENTS

★ ★ ★

INDEX TO POETS

INDEX TO ILLUSTRATORS

Artist	Page

Pitika Ntuli

THESE DAYS . . .

These days I converse with death
behind a funeral procession of ideas
a horse drawn cart gallops away with
coffins draped in bleeding shrouds

The funeral is postponed
I tease death
for keeping his landlord waiting

The earth yawns
its apertures stretch their rectangular
shapes in symmetrical lines
an epidemic of rash
moves to level the earth.

I converse with death these days
about a war of position
The state of affairs lies
within systems of fortresses
of earthworks

I question death's hegemony
I puzzle the dialectic of coercion and consent
death only smiles
I assess and re-assess the current situation
the balance of forces
of my organic crisis
unbalanced I threaten death with my death
He only smiles

Billy Childish

THE SONS OF MAN

because the past beckons
with cheap glamour
with memorys of the summer
of youth
and all is fragments and lies

because the future bites with
chill disdain
so it seems to each man
that he is born at an evil time

and as generation begats generation
and all dream past glorys
each age remembering only
the voices of its generals

love has been kindled and love lost
again and again
the fathers have forgotten their sons
and wretched it lives in the bossom
of every man
each little hart snagged on the
memory of a memory

so grasp instead this poisonous moment
each second tripping on the edge
of oblivion
and by this breath only
know that god is still bountyfull

(Billy Childish is dyslexic; this poem appears as written by the author.)

Laura Margolis

TO THE PERCEPTION OF THE SOUL

i arrived at an edge
where everything had melted
and the deep space of unknown particles
extended beyond all imagination

i stood in wonder
in awe of this thing called the universe
that exists without rhyme or reason
just simply and wholly inexpressible

    BACK TO REALITY
THIS ROOM
THESE WALLS
AND THE BLOCKS OF CONCRETE
        BRICK
        GRANITE
        STEEL
        STONE
        THAT SURROUND
           DARKENING THE SKYLINE

HELLO GREY MONDAY
    HIGH HEELS TAP ON PAVEMENT
    CAR WHEELS ON TARMAC
    THIS CITY WAKES EACH MORNING
    TO SOUNDS OF BONDAGE
        POLLUTION
        PIERCING THROUGH
           THESE PEACEFUL AURAS

blocked by science
silenced by control
i carefully u n r a v e l l e d every emotion
that had knotted inside

and the fine translucent threads of my soul came free
to drift rainbowed in warm aqua seas
scattered with the diamonds
of sparkling sunlight

and all i knew was
i did not own anything
yet
  it was all mine
  to perceive

Ashraf Mansoubivand

METAMORPHOSIS VERSUS PSYCHOSIS

The machinery of life
where even little sparrows
are messengers sent
by demons in outer space
is now turning into a spirit
breathing in and out
growing into tomorrow
finding shape
as life.

The ghosts of the city
who rule over
the theatre of my mind
repeating the play
in minute details
are now becoming memories
initiating
the dance of my spirit
spread in the eyes
of everywhere.

The darkness of heart
eats both inside and outside
seeing love
in a desperate hunger
filled with light
emanating from sounds
inside the silence.

The mirror shaking with fear
dissolves into a miraculous course of water.

FLIGHT OF THE SHAMAN

We lost the knack, the basic skill,
of how to speak like lizards and rocks;
smell colours; walk beneath the skin,
of others as well as our own.
Of how to sing with the voices of animals.
Nightshade berry eyes burning bright
around the fox-red fires of night.
We've been like astronomers
unable to see the milky way hidden by
the light pollution of consumerism.
The *you* usurped the *thou*.
Stone was killed stone dead.
We lost the knack but it's coming back.
Like a badger I dig for it
in the dark soil of our forgetting.
As a bird of prey hunts for its stolen voice
in the entrails of fieldmice and voles.
As sure as a woman's form was pulled
from forest flowers
and an owl pulled from the woman.
Soon I will exist in three worlds at once
and travel in nine.

Jeanette Ju-Pierre

TOTANKA TATANKA

Am I going to just sit here, defenceless,
a toothless ass, and watch you squirt urine
in my eyes?

Am I going to cry until I soak my land in
your fears, and wait for some miracle to wash
away your guilt?

Am I going to reach for my heart and dissect it,
demanding to know what part did fate play in
my land's flight into your hands?

Am I going to sleep until my dreams are
black and white, and refuse to find a solution
to my people's drink problem?

Am I going to laugh until my mind goes crazy,
hunting for some excuse to come down on your
conscience like an angry flight of pigeons?

Am I going to read about the buffalo and the bear
and hope that in those tales, I will find out
what happened to the Blackfoot tribe?

Am I going to learn how the power of faith has
a way of calming dead particulars because
my people do not have a future yet?

Or am I just going to sit through this life and
hope that some day the great spirit will return to
give us back our birthright! My people's land!

Debbie McNamara

THE HEALING STREAM

That coiled snake inside my belly
Resonates vicious fear
I touch it with my strong left hand:
Lurching, it retreats further up into my body

I try to get rid of it
It's heavy when I walk
I can't, I sit; I cry;
It smiles.

I go to the healing stream
With a woman close to my mother
In a cotton shift I lie in the waters
She puts stones on my belly

I am rocked by the water
I am a pool, an eddy
I am the rhythm of falling water
A million drops in an entity

The stones are washed away from me
Leaves are in my hair
Mara's hand is helping me
I am crying and laughing there

When the time is ready
I come back from the stream to the land
I shake a million drops from my shining form
I take the woman's hand.

Hilary Porter

BRIDE

Like a chrysalis she reclined,
the dream seemed lucid at the time –
seventeen, untouched by love,
he seemed to hover just above her mind.

She raised her troubled head
and said "You're welcome
to my icy bed, where I am forced
to lie alone in silken sheets,
as cold and dead as stone".

Though she would gladly have him stay
he paused awhile . . . then turned away
returning to the night from which he came.
The merest shadow on the blind –
a product of her dormant mind?
Vanished – and he hadn't left his name!

Each night she flung the windows wide
till darkness brought him to her side:
Silence, save the rustling of a tree.
The moment that she closed her eyes
he said "I've come to rescue you
from your virginity. Come, lie with me".

Offering her virgin neck,
a fleeting smile (just for effect)
she tried to draw him deep into her womb;
and yet she knew each time he came,
softly whispering her name
he'd take more of her life-blood to his tomb.

No-one can reach her now:
His face appears each night
through fluttering lace –
the curtains part
to freeze her heart
in the ice of his embrace.

The last time that he came to her
he said "I've come to rescue you
from your mortality –
come, fly with me".
and in that moment she became his bride.

Jenny Ford ————————————————

A CASE FOR SELF-ADVOCACY *post mortem*

Although Sylvia herself is dead
she's made again, over and over.
They take her and make her over, over
again and again. In their heads they shape
and fashion her and have her printed out,
more black than black on white, on paper.
It's always men, almost always, who mop up
where others have bled and make out
of being, doing; who make up a case
for themselves as mentor, progenitor . . .

She isn't Sylvia's Sylvia any longer,
she isn't herself now, she can't be.
Not so much as a shred of her breath remains
unswept up from the flat in Fitzroy Road:
the nursery's bare. In her garden, grown
over with brambles, mist hangs dankly round
the yew tree. It's all empty. Dull. From the earth
brown bed where her wounds lie, her words lie,
they keep on bleeding, we keep on reading
all the doing of her undoing.

Colin Hambrook ———————————————

WHEN THE SCISSORS CUT HER SKY

To die on "The Cross" was how Rose put it,
Intense yet vulnerable with her truth
That she was indeed a touchstone for the dead,
On their march to the failed light of oblivion.
Eternity had stalked her; seized the longing
And the love for life and squeezed
Every inch of time from her grasp;
Dried memory, till sucked and blown
She would call herself "Lady",
That life might assume a semblance of dignity.

To label her schizophrenic was misleading.
How she raged at the term
For the lie it made of her life.
When the scissors cut her sky
And heaven's hell-gates opened like a thief,
It was not her personality that split
But an external vibration that invaded her psyche
With meanings beyond the gate of imagination.

Sometimes the hi-jackers of her soul were friendly.
Talking, she would soothe their fears of being dead;
Have a laugh with being's inadequate shadow.
Occasionally, feelings of being raped;
The most horrific deaths, would ravage her body
Moving through, like a bullet with no destination.
Far from being weak, she forged a roaring will
To shake from her mind the disorientation and anger
Of souls refusing to accept the injustice of their deaths.

With a sense of resignation she reported
Being nailed to the cross many times.
Her burden was to spend a life time struggling
For a sense of separation from an impartial universe;
To have been clamped in the electric grip of a psychiatry
That is itself mentally sick with a fearful denial
Of the temporal realities of others' endurance.

Billy Childish

IN DEAD MENS SHOES

rite thru my teens i walked in
dead mens shoes
and slept in dead mens beds
on matresses of blud and
stains unknown

and we laughed
and we kissed
and we wept
no wonder that our sleep
was so often wondered by ghosts

and in the charity shops i would find
suit jackets with no trousers
a sure sign that this was the suit they
wore when they dropped

and sometimes there was a name tag
and other times not
just an egg stain on the lappel
and once a safty pin and a two bob bit

and never believing myself worthy of
anything new
i walked with the dead
and slept under their eaves
drinking from their cups
and eating from their plates
as if the poor were never burried

and if ever i find a penny in a pocket
i drop it in the nearest drain
vowing never to bow to its deadening eye
so being able to walk in dead mens shoes
and rid myself of ghosts

(Billy Childish is dyslexic; this poem appears as written by the author.)

EASTER

Four and bored
He fidgets prayer,
Would clockwatch
If he could,
Bouncing on and off
His pew
Is finally silenced
With a backhander
And "God's watching you !"

John Rety

I WISH YOU WERE HERE

Where I sit on the poor side of Burgos
       the sun at noon
With you NWest to my left shoulder
       somewhere between Norwich and London
Between my sitting form and the concourse
       of seven dials
A wedding party of finely dressed beautiful people
       Gold, black mantilla,
But simple, warm people not ashamed to sit in their finery,
Children in pink and blue, running to and fro
On a ledge leading to steps
The sign says: *Entrada Peatones* (must find out what it means)
While you are somewhere between Norwich and London
       not High Barnet, not Palmers Green
When the dice threw us Camden Town
Here at the wedding party,
       the laughter, the proud parents
       the excited children
In Norwich the funeral
       no doubt just as loving if sad
       But I hope even more comforting
As these faltering words
As faltering as the unknown stone carver's
       Smuggling in between the praying saints
       Himself and his companion coupling
And it is still there in the Museo de Burgos
       among all the guilt (oops: gilt!) and marble
       Unnoticed in the shadowy corner,
Talking of shadows, yesterday
       I saw a yawning soldier with his machine gun
       guarding the toy town barracks
On the wall a plaque with the best City and Guilds lettering
       So proud of that Caudillo
       ? What kind of *El Cambio* is this?
But this is a love poem
       and here it must end.

Jenny Corbett

RISING ABOVE IT

Oh yes, we all have them
Those times when irritation
Busts you right up
And you could tear apart
All mangy curs –
Raging against the injustice of it
Whirling you up inside.

Just rise above it
Lift your mind out
Let it float away
From all this crap
Leave go and skim
High on another plane.
Sometimes, believe me,

I rise so far
Touch soaring birds
Roll giddy into clouds.
Then nothing touches you
You breathe slow and deep
And only sink when ready.
Rising above is good for the soul
I recommend it.

Ray Willmott

ENCOUNTER

Wounds of a put-up christ
Won't save you,
Nor sufferings of another
Buy you heaven.

Innocent blood won't wash
On those unmapped roads
Of the heart, where no-one
Knows what the deal is,

Or what the hell the problem is
If you run into
Yourself and get taken
For a stranger.

Since, dying or travelling,
You'll still be who you are;
And when you see the face of god
It will always be your own.

Lynne Beel

ENTERED, NOT ON MY PERMISSION,
BUT THEIR CONSENT . . .

Curtains, curtains, billowing;
Ever centred in my mind,
Subject to the movement of the exercised
Hand to pass
Undaunted over the rails
On which the material, thick, heavy,
Falls;
Intentions built into silence exhausted.

Brought in on the splintered wheels of a
Mind-trolley blown, scenes unrecognisable
Melt and re-emerge before my
Dulled mind-bed.

Further: dead-pan
Curtains gently parted reveal
Eternity
Door-locked.

UNDER THE ASYLUM TREE

A prisoner in the asylum,
Said we were all trees,
I laughed,
Thinking that he meant we were all literally trees.

I thought
"They won't get to the roots of the problem,
We're starved of a positive environment."

Every ward was named after a tree.
Seeds were pills,
Branches were walls.

Sitting under the asylum tree.

Jade Reidy

DON'T GET ME WRONG

I'm not a real poet
I would think before I'd start,
these words that I'll be writing
are not a work of art.
they're just the way I'm feeling
they're my own way of dealing
with the messiness inside.

it took me years to find my voice
to believe I had a choice
and that rules were made for breaking.
this is what I learnt at the university –
Milton was for men and white misogyny
Sexton was a victim of psychiatry
Eliot predestined for immortality
along with Chaucer, Edgar Allen Poe and Percy B Shelley
and that was poetry?

I wrote my exam on a local Maori guy.
his poems were lyrical, angry
they made me want to cry
but the tutor wrote him off
for his mixed metaphor marked me down
and seriously chose to ignore
the passion.

but I know now what I suspected even then
that not all poets are white educated men.
their classical allusions
just creating mind confusions,
it's a hiding of the truth
so the poet stays aloof
from any raw emotion
but let me tell you brothers
and my sisters in the rhyme
it takes more guts to speak your heart
than to reveal a clever mind.

SINK CITY

My blank goldfish eyes
Stare past the beaded window
To another world
Lying far and beyond
Sink City,
Then slowly drop
Into my milky bowl
Where a thousand fairy eyes
Wink up at me,
But their flattery cannot help.

Lost upon a wave,
I feel myself drowning
In a frothy sea
Of mealtime remnants
That bob about my ears
Like so much giddy flotsam,
And I taste the wet boredom
Of sailing cornflakes
Cruising in lip harbour.

As I empty the bowl
My head breaks the surface
Submarine style,
Lungs gasping for breath
Needing release
From the very greyness of it.
And standing in the corner
Plug in hand,
The hoover leers
And mocks my insanity.

Martin Henderson

PATIENT NUMBER 16543 C

(Inspired by reading *The Catch of Hands*,
an autobiography, by Benedicta Leigh)

Was it really fifteen summers
Fifteen winters
Fifteen years ago –

When the certainties of my young life
Dissolved
I trusted no-one.
And the sense I had
Of nothing again
Being straightforward
Or simple.
As I waited in line
For medication
Or sat in the day-room
Concentration blown.

And the family visited
Every day
And friends came too.
But could not reach me.

One evening, I ran
Out of the hospital
Across outlying ground
. . . And finally was picked up
By a policeman in a Panda Car.

All this I recapture –
I thought it would never
Could never
Come out all right
In the end.

D.I.Y.

Dear Miss Do-it-all D.I.Y. Home Improvements,
You have mended hearts
Built shelters
Kept the stairs safe
Bandaged bleeding wounds
Constructed solid units
Creosoted barriers
Built the garden wall
Made your mother happy
Planted tomorrow's cabbages
Made them chicken soup
Shored off vacuums
Replenished the empties
Bought the right Christmas presents
Looked on the bright side
Donated your organs to science
Syphoned off the filth
Re-charged the batteries
Effected the essential plumbing
Kept secrets
Stopped them from going mad
Oiled the wheels of fortune
Made the bed comfortable
Considered his point of view
Pumped deflated egos
Sugared the bitter pill
Camouflaged the monsters
Brandy-buttered the stale pudding
Nailed down loose partitions
Saved for the rainy day
Kept the world at bay
Created the nourishing brew

Dear Miss Do-it-all D.I.Y. Home Improvements
(who stopped them from going mad)
Tell me,
What is there left for you?

Mike Burrows

WINTER NIGHT

The wind cried like a baby – no-one here
running, hushing to feed, to wipe, to stroke
and hug that child, to enfold it from fear
of nameless discomforts, and dark that broke
on dream-lit head, a dark sudden as light
that lifted and smacked it, forced it to wake,
to breathe, eat, need cleaning, five-sense tonight
unamnioned, a breastless, sundered ache.
Terror in waves, not the waves within Her,
breakers needed as he stands on grey shore
loved, then alone, with face to the brined air –
but the nerve-waves that burn him, only more
open each time he stiffens – so staring,
a-writhe – wet bed, spiked roof-reeds up-bearing.

———Ashraf Mansoubivand———

INTOXICATION

My salvation is in a gross belief
The belief that mirrors distort
And my self is more beautiful
Than the image my mirrors reflect
After all others are distorted by mirrors
My eyes are my mirrors
I trust my left eye more than my right
But my eyes choose to see
They have minds of their own
When intoxicated
By these atmospheric waves
All the mirrors disappear
And time becomes a mirror itself
Then I see famous people
In famous situations
Creating famous tomorrows
Then I feel I have entered a mirror
And those who are watching through us
Are writing the action of the present
Then I fear I may suffocate in the mirror
Hearing bells and thinking
I can understand the birds
But how do the bells know?
Then I realise I am only
Experiencing what is called madness
Then I am also safe.

Joe Bidder

COWARD

    . . . . . . you flinched
from walking the road
paved with flint,
strove instead to pose
on polished boards
to gain significance,

but the wind disallowed
that moment of ecstasy,
cast you down
to taste failure;

so you hid
played games
buried spiritual ambitions
in the tomb of cynics,

but the wind is fickle
ghosts, then storms
indiscriminately
beyond calculation,

forces confrontation
rams home truth
makes you face
the mirror
where you must
submit.

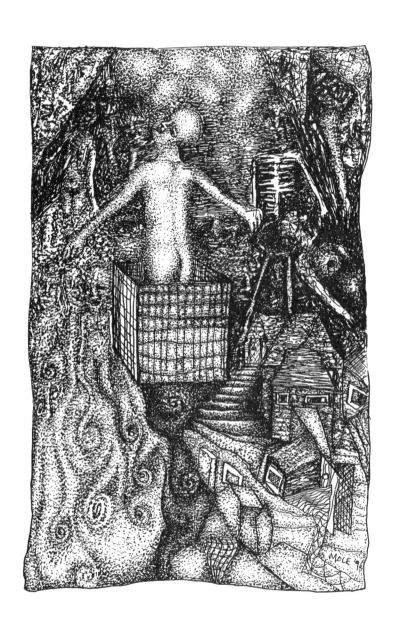

Patrick McManus ————————————————

GREAT DAY, FOR MY SUICIDE!

had a good run, can't complain
but enough is enough, life's a strain
a grand finale, or a quiet exit?
pills are easy, but a bit passé
cutting arteries, in baths messy,
jumping out of tall buildings
not as reliable as it's cracked up to be
starving to death has a certain style
but needs time, and space and guile
remember to leave the phone off the hook
and notes on door "gone an holiday"
pop down to the library, for information
ask librarian for suicide diy
tips on writing that last note
how do you build an electric chair?
strength of rope, drop for hanging?
which are the best, gasses or poisons?
a crucifixion is tricky single-handed!
yes make a list, get it together
this time tomorrow, gone forever
great day for my suicide!

ACTING LIKE A MADMAN

Is this really me, here, now,
acting like a madman
(if madmen there be)?
In this absurd one-person show;
an impromptu street-theatre
where the audience stops to stare
awhile in wonder,
before rushing on
without a clap,
at this performing clown – who's me.
Without any make-up
real blushes show.
Must I attract these crowds,
humiliate myself.
wave arms, do odd gestures,
exhibit on this frightening public stage
with no learnt lines,
just prompted cues
from some inner conflict
which makes me panic in this mad way.
Must I hold the stage so readily,
like a court jester,
have people chuckle, laugh and point
at this enigma – who's me,
performing like a madman
(if madmen there be)?

LEAVING HOSPITAL

Five months inside
the shell of a Work-House/Asylum:
sixty years to paint over
the smell of cruelty and innocent faces
they jammed between the bricks.

I want to be an undercoat for a little longer
and tell dirty jokes to the nineteenth
century.

They're forcing me out
into Now.
Into an upside-down,
inside-out Gulliver's world.

Where everything's changed:
the streets, the cafes, the toilets.

Judy Kessler

OLD SONG TITLES

It's been a lousy week
And my voice has said
Put it behind you now, the thieving I mean.
Yet I still feel hurt and angry inside.
The Establishment send them in
And sure, I need them to help me cope.
I'm different now and wonder how long
It takes to come to terms.
When I feel stressed I think of the past
Bathing days: how sensuous –
How long – how my body tingled
With life's energy!
But now with fleeting time's care
I feel at times unknown, like an animal,
Just plunged in to be cleansed
Of vermin and stench!
I am the good ol' gal
Who tries to make it all better
by saying no one's to blame.
Yet, I think of my Mother
Who sent me the gift
Hidden away in its soft plastic bed,
Fifty quid gone walkabout
Like the frozen bird coming to life
Singing to the cash, come fly with me.
So I'll put it behind me now
And accept that some people
Come into your life
And then *s-t-e-a-l* away home.

Eamer O'Keeffe ─────────────────

SWINGS AND ROUNDABOUTS

I chartered a flight with Quintas,
took out a loan with Edrisal,

floated in space with Feminax,
built a new world on Volidan,

flayed myself with Flagyl,
got expansive with Stilboestrol,

short-circuited with Luminol,
bled for Amenerone,

was tangled up by Melleril,
broken down by Stelazine,

sleep-walked all day by Largactil,
locked in jail by Librium,

went loco chasing Lomotil,
cooked my goose with Tetrazine,

slept with Phenobarbitone,
got hyper with Valium,

went numb with Distalgesic,
mortgaged a wall with Ativan,

raved all night with Mogadon,
survived with Temazepam.

SOMETHING RATHER PECULIAR HAPPENED TODAY.
I GOT UP RATHER LATE AND . . .

Something rather peculiar happened today,
I got up rather late,
But could still see myself lying there,
As I sat and watched myself,
I saw my life rising up and up,
Until my mind exploded like a volcano,
Spewing forth past, present and fiction in one almighty mass.
It felt strange watching it all escaping,
After being locked away for so many years.
Anti-social and on the run,
A fugitive I never thought I'd have to meet,
And all in one mad uncontrolled moment it's here,
I wanted to move, turn away, block it out,
But I couldn't,
Rather like the "Singing Detective",
Lying there, thinking back,
And substituting fantasy for pain,
As it all roared and spluttered,
I knew I couldn't cry,
The things that so long had lain dormant were now on the loose,
I shielded myself, not wanting to let them touch me.
The heat became intense,
Like an inferno,
But I knew once it had burned itself out,
It would just become ash,
Blown away by the wind,
With no chance of getting back.
Something very peculiar happened today,
And all I could do was laugh.

YOU COULD ALREADY BE A WIENER

I like to go out . . . Way out . . .
Where it's deep . . . Really deep.
Where if you're not careful you might not come back.

I like to get really abstract . . . on the fringes,
Where colour and objects mean nothing . . .
And feeling means everything.

Everything is crazy out here . . . Way out here.
Where the ice is thin . . . Maybe too thin . . .
And the candle burns, Both ends nearing the centre.
And the thread is ready to snap . . .
And your ten million dollar check could already be in the mail.

LULLABY

I'm thinking of a lullaby
So that when the nurse comes round
I can sing it to myself
And not be frightened of the sound
Of feet, clacking across the floor
And click of catch, and creak of door.

I keep my head tucked in the bed
And hold my breath.

The drums are beating in my ears
As a stealthy tread draws near
And hear the silence sear the night
As torchlight strikes its yellow beam
Upon the pillow where my head has been.

This is how the nurses keep us
Feeling safe in a short night's sleep.

Susan O'Brien————————————————

A CLINICAL DEPRESSION

I want to ask what
chance there is
of getting some time
off for good behaviour
but know the answer's none.

And failures from the past
have taught me that
escape attempts
will be no use at all,
and lead only to an
increase in my term.

And so I plead my innocence
instead and ask, as each
of us must do,

The never-ending question
"Why – and if no freedom
  now – then when?"

Johnny Crescendo

TAKING MY LEG OFF AT NIGHT MEANS

When I take my leg off
I've finished!
When I take my leg off
That's it
When I take my leg off
I do not want to be reminded that I've left my lights on in my
car which is parked thirty yards down the street
because some bastard has parked in my reserve place
and who will be quite nice and gentle about it
in the morning when I confront him
but will remain in my eyes
a bastard for evermore.

When I take my leg off
It means freedom
When I take my leg off
It's my choice
When I take my leg off
I take off the scaffolding and knots that have bent and broken
me in cringing embarrassment and I tell all the collaborators
to fuck off and go counsel themselves.

When I take my leg off
It's a simple act
an' I'm used to it
When I take my leg off
Nobody can tell me what to do
Or does
When I take my leg off
I can get away from the world of the medics and the do-gooder
and imagine that the world was born at the same time I was and
I am here by right because my parents wanted me to be here.

Rosemary Norman————————

EATING DISORDER

I am the bone, sufficient.

Whatever is soft in you, and wants comfort,
I bite deep into it.

I work from the inside out. I expose you
slowly as one of my own.
You grow thinner.

Now you will not relent. Once
you lapped up anything.
Discrimination? You licked its edges
smooth and creamy,
your mouth was a blur, there were crumbs
between your fingers.
Later they'd hurt like grit.

Let your last breath lift you, light
as dust into the nostrils
of sleek and slippery eaters.
I will coat their tongues with you.

But the skin still clings,
and a little movement
of fever in your sockets tells me
you have an eye still, for the blubbery world.

Val Stein —————————————————————

AFTER ALL, THEY ARE SIZE SIX AND A HALF

I went to the hospital
The consultant said
The problem with my feet
was all in my head.

Well I'd say that my feet
wouldn't fit in my head
but he said they're in there
and he's the med.

But after some measuring
had taken place
I realised they might just fit
right in his face.

Anna Louise

HAIR CARE

I dyed you black
in the depression
I permed you to look fifteen
you went purple with psychiatric trauma
and green when the dye failed
you shone
dark red and honey blonde
shaved
half crazed
at the unemployment queue
you were cut
like income support
and grown for vanity but
your ends are split
like a schizophrenic

Judy Kessler

I WORRY SOMETIMES

I worry sometimes
When Mand goes to London
To see her Dad
And I'm alone and it's cold.

I worry sometimes
That I easily fall
And the mountains stairs beckon me
To hot tea.

I worry sometimes
That the cat might crap
And the Home Help
Have to clean up the carpet.

I worry sometimes
That I might be in another home,
Not my home,
But in the home of other old women
With dry wombs
Who worry sometimes
That they are a worry.

DAISY

daisy is disturbed
doesn't do as the doctor ordered
dances barefoot down the lane
dashes cataclysmic
irrationally rhythmic
with a leaping, bounding madness
no psychiatrist can name

they gave her a label
she peeled it off and ate it
they gave her another
she burnt it in the fire
they gave her a cure
for the tiger in her throat
for the wasp in her spleen
for the scorpion in her stomach
for the serpent in her eyes

she pours their potions down the sink
she drowns their warnings with her cries
she dances barefoot down the drive
it isn't done, it isn't seen
it isn't clean, it isn't nice
it isn't what the doctor ordered
isn't what the judges want
it's cold and hard and frightening
it shakes the world and makes it dance
it takes the sun and burns it black
it makes the night seem even darker
than the darkness in our hearts

it reminds us of ourselves

daisy is disturbed
with a spinning-top dementia
that spins and spins and will not stop
that shakes the world and makes it dance
that rattles and screams
that spits and cries:

I am alive

TOILET POETRY

There are five buttons
Between me and my leak
If I can't do the buttons
I'm straight down shit creek

What use is a paddle
If your fingers just fumble?
What use is a hand
If your fingers turn bland?

Forget about buttons
I've taken my leak
And left them a puddle
For those up shit creek!

Ian Jentle

COMMUNITY CARING

Lumbering homeward
Burdened with bags
Tapping through crowds
Like a clockwork lobster
I heard a woman's voice
Hoarse with dementia
Enraged, deranged
Angered and endangered
She must have sighted on my stick

"You're not fucking blind!" she screamed
"I'm fucking blind. You're not fucking blind,
   You're deaf you fucking fake you fuck you fucker!"

Foaming with fury
She dogged me through the flinching crowds
I felt their fear
I tasted their distaste

I should have joined her screaming
"Take care community
   The carnival is coming
   Come and see the rejected
   The neglected and subjected
   Come and join our parade of profanities
   Let's all do the cursing conga

   A-bugger arsehole shit, fuck!
   A-bugger arsehole shit, fuck!"

But I didn't
And they wouldn't
I plodded on my homeward path
Deserted by my raging acolyte
Who abandoned her assault
Distracted by somebody's dog.

BUT I DON'T WANT A DOG

"You should get a dog" they said
"It must be easier being led
  Than groping in the dark.
  Think of walks in the park!
  And what about muggers
  And those other buggers
  That muck you about
                When you go out.

  You'd meet more people
  A dog breaks the ice
                and that'd be nice
  For you
  Living alone
        Like you do."

  I do understand
  How a dog in the hand
  Can be a friend
  And can lend
  A real assistance
  To sightless existence

  But

  If I do crave company
  Golden-haired and longing to lick me,
  It is definitely not
  Of the canine variety
  Not everybody likes
  Walking behind
  A labrador's bum
  I know that some
  Are thrilled to bits
  With their furry chum
  But to me
  It's just a stick
  That shits.

Lynne Beel

THE COMMUNITY CENTRE
(. . . . *survivorwitz*)

Late, that thickish night,
Slouching down the brick-walled City avenue,
A soulless domain . . . . no shadow of being
Or solid form to invade;
Nonetheless, I am brought to attention
By a vast light suddenly switched-on
As if from a remote socket high-up
In the murky heavens.

From a dull alleyway
Into the lumbered moonlight
Step two grey-dressed men
In peaked caps with a pair of sleek
Canines ambling sedately along.

They cross the road down front
And looking upwards I see above
Clustered searchlights grouped
Over the nearby high-walled arena.
Through a security entrance,
Anonymously coded,
The men disappear.

But I must hurry. To the yellow-beamed
Light from the swing doors
Of a multi-windowed hut at the
Street's end. Walk in, half shadowed
Past the "Razor-wire, beware".

See dimly an old burner down the back,
Already a bar or two singeied out.
Candle flickers. Row, faces, rows.
At every hand on table
A thin sheet lies.

Songs, recitation,
Tinged with the warmth of
Momentary gratitude.
Outside;
What soul to step down the razed moonlight?
Decipher the coding in the streets;
Raise again a rifle, unsuspect.

PLAYMATES

Music is the dance of life
and rhythm is the key
I have a good sense of rhythm
will you play with me?
Let my hands bow you firmly
finding low tones
of pleasure
fingers noting your valves
that pulse with my pressure
I want to palm your drum bum
slicing a slap that reverberates
pluck the strings
of your harp
slip my tongue seductively
over your mouthpiece
and suck in the air
ready to get high
notes
I won't come
to you in C sharp, B flat
or even major chords
just the rhythm pulsating
insistent
willing to touch
your music setting
my sex a-dancing
as my fingers run
along the cadences of your keyboard

Scott Verner

AN AUDIBLE IMAGE
(To D D)

Elliptic and sharp as an eyelid,
your poems incise penumbras,
bleeding shadow juice on star tissue
to clench night vision like an audible mirage.
Retinas flicker eclipses.
You blink my mind and I flinch, forward.

Hugely infinitesimal,
with black hole mass and density,
your poems filament nets of dark matter
trawling all of us and inexistence.

Like kisses, your words' soft frictions incandesce
to silhouette the sun's euthanasia,
incantating verges of visibility,
calibrating eyes of time,
elucidating recondite light
and curving perspective like an hour.

In dawn twilight I sight your images
like Capella and Sirius
without shades in internal celestial mirrors
to kiss horizons of enlightenment
and fix my Estimated Position.

Your poems make invisibility
a sight to see.

David Pelling————————————

GIRLFRIEND

I have seen thee fish! No! Be still! come close!
I have seen thee snare the coot as it fed
And take the screaming kestrel as it soared.
With all thy might thou throwest thy bread at trees,
And when the float doth sink thou singst a song.
This all London knows; I speak the truth
Thou knowst I flatter not, my winsome Ruth
Yea, I have seen thee fish, would know thy art.
The which, not known, is lost if we should part.
I have seen thee fish, yet not seen thee catch.
Caught only moanings as the midges hatch,
Or dull groanings when this year's tiddlers snatch;
Sought thee at dusk to hear thee curse the gnat,
Or shriek at beetles crawling where thou sat,
Come closer! We two could such tangles make,
Would put to shame the very nests of birds!
I cannot claim I fish with equal art,
('Twas first thy fishy skill that stole my heart)
For thou hast stunned the living bird in flight
And taken trees where no trees lay in sight.
All this and more must be thy task to teach.
I am not proud . . . . . .

Richard McKane

A J

"What a way to spend the night
before your birthday – in a police cell"
"Now," he said "all I can do is write."
And then he produces his list of convictions.

He smells of stale cider and rotting straw.
I'm not sure which Islington Restaurant
he ate his meal in and didn't pay.
Sectioned in a mental hospital, due for discharge
on Monday, he phoned P3 to ask
if his latest exploit would stand against him.
A little petty shoplifting, the free Restaurant game,
experienced
chasing the dragon, a bit of weed,
a snort or two – and the psychotropics,
administered over ten years: stelazine,
chlorpromazine (the Russian aminazine), fluphenazine
decanoate - the 4 Zines. And a novel.

It was a birthday in his thirties.
We had lunch together in my Council Flat.
Campbell's chicken stew and Heinekens,
but it was somehow more than that:
two unbroken brother writers breaking bread.

*(Andrew John McKane, author of the novel **A Feast of Beggars**
[Dunscaith 1990]died on 1st December 1994 of a heart attack. He was 41.)*

Sean Gilligan

EMMA

Emma drinks champagne from velvet green bottles
Emma eats mountains of snow-capped chocolate
Emma skates on Christmas-card ice
Emma dances on strawberry Pavlova
Emma sits in a gossamer armchair
Emma sleeps on a cotton wool cloud
Emma cries tears of dry white wine
Emma makes love without feeling a thing.
Emma was probably born under Pisces –
at least she always wanted to be hooked.
Someone should catch her before she drowns.
Emma, take off my velvet green jacket;
Emma, throw away the horse-rider's whip.
Emma, don't listen to cathedral bells –
hear the torment you cause in our souls.
Let's weep on our shoulders; give yourself to me.
No more recrimination, no more masturbation.
Emma, look at your reflection in my eyes –
I don't love you, you don't love me,
but we're both in love; we're both fantasies.
Shall we weep alone together? –
or shall we realise our dreams?

Paul Gerhard

COMEUPPANCE

"I'm up!" "Don't worry, you'll just go down,"
She says, I face her for the worse.
"I'm down!" "Don't worry, you'll soon come round."

So I'm aroused, and quite spell bound:
I'd dare to date this sexy nurse?
"I'm up!" "Don't worry, you'll just go down."

That dig downbeats this horny clown.
My toy of feel could get no worse.
"I'm down!" "Don't worry, you'll soon come round."

I lust to nip her off, up town,
Could steal the strings on my poor purse.
"I'm up!" "Don't worry, you'll just go down."

My mind's eye bares her undressed down.
"D'you fancy an intrepid date?"
I ask. "That's inappropriate

Behaviour," she standoffish states.
"I'm down!" "Don't worry, you'll soon come round."
Revolving off, I hit the ground.

She says: "Get up!" "Up where? You've turned
Me down!" "Don't worry, you'll soon come round."
"I'm up!" "Don't worry, you'll just go down."
"I'm down! I know: You want me round!"

Isha

WHEN

When I was at the nadir
Of my volcanic pit
Too far beneath
The reaching hands at crater's edge

You phoned me
regularly
And you said,
"How are you?"

I was not well enough to lie
Nor to prevaricate,
nor deal in simple greetings;
Too distressed to describe my state
I mumbled weakly, "Help me, please help me."

You never visited, consoled nor fed me,
Never changed my clothes,
Never washed up, nor bathed me, nor took me for a walk;
You never sought assistance for me.

You rang, you said,
Because you worried –
that you'd feel guilty
if you didn't ring me.

So when I was at my lowest ebb
You rang to assuage your guilt
And now you know I'm much improved
I hear you'd like to meet again.

David Pelling

A QUIET DIVORCE

The moon slipped alliteratively through the clouds,
Clouds puffed up with sheaves of simile,
While the trees,
Hung in metaphoric shrouds,
Drooped under the weight of overripe hyperbole
Wordless moon, cloud and tree,
What can you mean to me?
Word, moon, cloud and tree,
Jubjub, chung-chung, bubblegum, bee.

Sunset comes in a whisper
Wordlessly.
No need to paint or draw
A visitor on the shore
Of time, I feel the ebb tide
Pulling through the flood of wonder.
I grow older,
And the solid earth will crowd
With life unborn:
Speechless I await
The gibberish of dawn.

ANGEL LOVER

I gave my angel lover
My slightly crumpled heart
We whispered words to the effect
That we would never part

We pledged to love each other
For all our natural life
He – the devoted husband
I – the cherished wife

I'll always love you, dear, he said
You are ingrained in me
Our lives are meshed together
Our love was meant to be

Time passed – we had some children
O happy wife and mother
Then one day my mate said to me
Dearest – I love another

It won't make any difference
To us, my angel swore
It isn't that I love you less
Just that I love her more.

Alex Benjamin

SURFACE IMPRESSIONS

A smile is painted
On the mask-like surface of my face

As if immortalised
By the skill of an artist's hand

I am shaped in your image
Of what a woman should be

And consent to be the object
Of your gaze

As I am nothing
If not forever versatile

Isha ————————————————————————

A SUITABLE TIME

Harry
Rings me
Every Thursday at three
To pester me
For my week's history.
Do I feel
Sad, very sad or not
Sad at all?

Is life
Worth living?
Carbohydrate craving?
Ate more? Put on weight?
Felt Guilt?

Then he want's to know –
Do I think about sex, he sez?
Do I think about the opposite sex?
(Last week he had the cheek
To tell me I don't know what I'm missing when I said, "no".)
No, I sez

What this is all about
– these telephone calls –
they are for my research
on impertinence
and the psychiatric nurse's aptitude
for reading questions from a sheet of paper.
Craftily,
I let him foot the phone bill.

James Turner

SOLO

It must be easy – *I* was never taught.
It's stopping that's hard. Not enough, to dread
the aftermath of love short-circuited,
the lassitude, the shame. You're fairly caught.

Still harder, now it's ceased to be a sin
– a fact you first learned from your therapist.
Most people do it, recent surveys say.
A sin? Oh no, it's just a nerve-machine
driven by natural lust in partnership
with most unnatural frustration. Why,

don't priests and monks do it? You always knew it
wasn't a sin, this warmth of liquid squeezed
from fevered flesh, the hungry gods appeased
so cheaply. Chimpanzees in zoos do it.

Mike Lawson

RISKY BUSINESS

To love and be loved must be the greatest thing
It can help you survive internment camps and loony bins
But it is a risky business

I learned this as I fed Largactyl to the pigeons

What happens when we lose love?
There is no good market for it
Is it coincidence or destiny
That made us recipients of psychiatry?
Did we sin to deserve all this, or is it an accidental kiss?
The greatest danger is to lose will
Then to be cast adrift with no depot of ambition
Except the psychiatrist's stare with the injection
And to take another pill
To be loved makes some of us feel important
Simply because we are loved
But what happens when there is an iron fist in the velvet glove?
Oh! misery
It is said it is better to have loved and lost
Than never to have loved at all
The trouble is that you know what you are missing
Especially if your loved one is off with your friend
It can drive you round the bend
Everything worthwhile is a risky business

I learned this as I fed Largactyl to the pigeons

They stumbled towards me the next day
And demanded Kemadrin
So gross national product
Is considered more important than happiness
As moon beams play on the incoming tide
It was just too good to be in that village in love
You had the keys to the door
I suppose you had to lock me out; or did you?
I am left with a shopping basket in Sainsbury's

POISON IN ITS KISS

Love is betrayed with a kiss
Sorry to say that it is
Weeping because its soul
Knew that kiss from days of old
Love is another exile
Banished for a while
Now begins that long
Night of tragic song.

Love is in touch with those
Who savour the smell of a rose,
Warning honest men
To beware of a new gospel
In the market place,
It's converting all at such a pace,
they're all on their knees,
They're praying and they all believe.

Love is in tears over young
Lovers kissing guns
'cause yesterday they said
They were going to be wed,
Now they are on the loose
With those guns and the gospel truth
They're hugging oblivion
That's their holy mission.

Love is aroused to say
Never, never, never obey
Those who hold up that sign,
For sale, all mankind
Stand up and raise your voice
Now is the time to make that choice
Choose a world where love
Doesn't have to be gospel.

Love is betrayed,
I heard there was poison in its kiss
Poison in its kiss.
Love is betrayed,
I heard there was poison in its kiss
Poison in its kiss.

THE USES OF POETRY

(Neither the scientist,
Nor his friends. . . .)

The Devil is in peril
Of being seen to be
Serious, actually; already
The night-jars jammed –
The eyes battened to a
Gaze locked in winks gone
Beyond forty.
I can't envy
The poor soul glumly
Sat on a restless stool –
Mr. Ego the Editor's
Left behind in his office of
Spent emotion a pile of
Thrown-away paper
He's never going to print or read.
Fetch one now for the Devil
To ease out a crease
In the smile
Of a short stanza.

Brian Docherty ─────────────────────

VIRTUOSO: JOHN OGDON, 1937-89

At nineteen we knew all about music
genius was Ray Charles or Pete Townshend
in our electric world Clapton was God.

Sunday night was suit-time in the *Golden Eagle*
learn to behave, drink Pernod and whisky
little *bhikkus* trying the world for size.

Then our inscrutable well-connected friend
brought a special guest to augment our sangha
enormous round *Bodhisattva* showing Right Speech.

He came among us like the blue-eyed stranger
with no history that we knew of
and a famous name that meant nothing to us.

By the exaggeration of respect, Mr John Ogdon
could have been a 33° Mason to provincial boys
untried at measuring beyond our own horizon.

Nobody guessed the long exile in the Maudsley
the piano a therapy tool between brainfrying sessions
editing out false notes in the mind's chatter.

The piano was always in the corner
an instrument of fixed and equal temper
solid and reliable in a world of shadows.

Fifteen years later he looked just the same
shuffling onto his Birthday Concert stage
a holy fool seated at his shrine.

Now he has walked to cold mountain,
his music is the light of the full moon,
a gift of clear water to guide the traveller.

Eamer O'Keeffe

MANDALA

I might escape
through this red
heart shape;

coil my thinking
in a spiral to still
my chaos.

I can match your
madness if you
tell me how
to get through.

Ricardo Corvalan

NOT DRUNK JUST LEGLESS

I

As a child I was always falling.
All part of growing up.

The bloody knees and broken limbs
Were familiar almost necessary.

But this was different.
A different kind of falling.

That first time
The floor simply fell away in silence
Like a globe spinning off its axis

And I thought it a cruel joke
Laughing furiously at my clumsiness.

II

You came to me
With your eyes full of longing
Smiling at the muted slapstick silence
And tried to get me up

But couldn't.

III

Falling is easy now.

Second nature.

Just relax and let the floor
Cushion the fall.

Now you too have a habit
The daily routine of washing
And getting me dressed

A simple but poor substitute
For the intimacy of love

And when the phone rings
For what seems an eternity
You imagine all kinds of new horrors

Me tumbling down the stairs
Or some broken bones.

IV

In the middle of the night
I feel your breasts press heavily
Against the lustful arch of my back

And under the light of your nipples
I secretly count fresh bruises.

Diane Pungartnik————————————

NULL AND VOID

Like flesh torn
from the bone
not cleanly
cut with knife
but shredded
bit by bit
you from my
side were ripped

I cried in my sleep last night;
this time the tears really came.
What terrible things happened
in the dream I don't recall,
only that I was sobbing
harshly and when, half asleep,
my hand crept up to my face,
I felt the wet and wondered.
Mama, I'm tired; my sad eyes
are calling. I can't go on.

As the man said My mind
is in darkness Holding
on for dear life   Too much
talk it's no good no good
Shadows under my eyes
You look so tired   God
how stupid can they get.

It is beyond interest
No tear or searing pain
Just a soft, dark nothing
Not fit to talk about

Each kiss will be the last,
each smell last forever.
But with each heady draught
Comes the desire for more.

My nose clings to your scent
I suck your fragrant skin.
So afraid I'll forget
What you were when you're gone.

Heather Parr

TANIA'S POEM
(Written to my mother)

You wanted a china doll.
They gave you a baby.
You broke the china doll –
She was too fragile for you.
You dropped her on the concrete floor
and broke her head in two.

The china doll cracked . . .
And the baby cried.

Daddy gave the doll away
to someone who could mend her.
Your baby girl was here to stay
with nowhere you could send her.
But in your mind the doll had died;
And in her cot the baby cried.
You couldn't recognise the pain
from emptiness inside.

The china doll is mended.
Another child can hold her.
Your baby grew – away from you.
You were afraid to touch her
in case you spoiled her;
maybe broke her.
Now that childhood's ended,
And you want her friendship
And think a smile will do
To mend the fragile cracks that grew
inside her mind
when love was scarce
and life was too unkind.

A china doll can feel no pain.
Its painted face is smiling.
But in your daughter's grown-up mind
There's still a baby crying.

A LESSON *(for Linda)*

Teacher paces out
The afternoon

Note this.

Note that.

Learn by heart
For Monday

One child
Pounced on explains
"Seagulls talk to me."

A controlled burst
Of laughter
From the class

"Oh yes
  And what do they say?"

"It's in seagull,"
The child replies
Then adding patiently
"And it's no good
  In English – doesn't rhyme!"

More laughter
But less this time.

I'M JUST HELPING DAD

See the children
Glued to the promise of money
See the children . . .
They have already learned
That love is a luxury
They cannot afford

Their keen eyes focus on the pound
In my pocket

But it's just business as usual
(A killer in disguise),
Business has torn all the wonder
From their eyes
A machine starts to live
Curiosity dies . . .

Business has torn all the wonder
From their eyes!

Terry Simpson

ANSWER

Pushing my sleeping child through the mist
I thought of what you'd said
the night we were drunk –

> 'Five years more, probably less,
> the species is finished, and hope a leap of faith;
> life is brutality, ignorance, boredom,
> talk of love a confidence trick;
> in flight from death
> we're all just looking for stimulation,
> betraying, surviving, our lovers dying
> in chambers we've helped to plan,
> and everything else is illusion for fools.'

I couldn't answer then,
and later on the bus
I'd still no words of refutation
– until my son's head rolled
against my neck and cheek
and I smelt the dust and soap and warmth of sleep.

Judy Kessler

THE WILL

I saw myself pinned up
Beside your mirror's reflection,
A younger woman
Surrendering up her past.
It is your choice not to see too much
Or think too much –
Except the right things to do.
One day, death's duster will polish off your
cardboard, Mother,
Into the flame's apricot laughter,
And there it will burst into a blue joke,
A familiar black comedy called, "Motherhood",
That leaves you everything to find in yourself.

Ifigenija Zagoricnik-Simonivic ——————

I USED TO BE A GIRL

One day my stepfather decided to strangle me.
He took care of me, then. He was taking me, then.
He had me ever since we moved into his house.
He took care of me, then. My mother said, I was
lucky. Not all stepfathers love their stepdaughters.

To strangle me was quite alright. I did indeed
miss the bus. I did indeed have sand in my schoolbag.
I did indeed forget to learn the rhymes. I did indeed
fail to be good, Oh, I did, my mother said, I was
lucky. Not all stepfathers are concerned.

No, I did not mind being strangled at all.
I only felt wrong about doing him a favour.

My mother was standing by, watching, holding hands
ready to catch me, later. Afterwards. She was going to
catch me, I knew I could trust her.

I looked at her face and I looked at his face
and the faces blended into a blurry patch of coloured
mist and cloud. Only their eyes were peeking through
like beams, hot rays making my throat dry and sore.

I could not stop thinking. I was visualising the day
before. He was handling me. He was saying not to be
scared. He needed me, he said. He washed his congealed
milk out of my hair just on time. I told my mother that
I was wet because my baby brother pissed into my face.
We all laughed.

I am here now. Still here. I am
looking forward to the final blow. I am indeed looking
forward into the future. I am lucky. I have no daughter.
I would find it hard to hold hands out ready to catch her.

ABSENCE

What shall I do
it's a chair
with three legs and a rung gone
What shall I do

A well-worn chair and Windsor
spray-back spindled caught svelt
splendidly eager
and dappled in time

Old chair
smiles me a tale
welcoming many a passing earthling
the lovingly-crafted
amply rounded plank
lent full support
all degree of weight
solitary hours of trial
contemplations of day and night
and in companionship took good share
accommodating the lean of years.

Seemingly
a chair
leans
from the feint corner of my room

There
no mere chair

Object
to bear the brunt of
human passions
caught up for many a knot of reason
cn cross-fire

Monument
to the Battle for Reality

Souvenir
of the Battle for Identity

A Son's
victim of anguish
seeking way

A chair
mere object
well-used
at random
a chopping-block for pain

There?
   Barely a Chair
      ghostly tauntings of yesteryear
         gildings
Narrative of dust and ashes

This is what bonfires are made for.

Martin Henderson

A DEATH IN THE FAMILY

"This is beyond justice, beyond comparing –"
(Libby Houston, "At the Mercy", Allison & Busby, 1981)

My mother cared for him at home, near the end
He had no illusions. Surrounded by the machinery
Pumps and drips and catheters: morphine for the pain.
Though his dying was a matter of hazy continuous dreaming
His manner of dying was sad, the loss of control, dealt with,
Passive. I went back to my job, shackled to misery
Amongst goldenrod and begonias and sympathetic colleagues.
And at last the expected phone call came.

We sang "Fight the Good Fight" at the funeral
Then in unaccustomed black blazer I handed out drinks.
Now his stamp collection and razor remind me daily
What I have lost, though we argued often: I miss most
His firm handclasp at Cardiff Station
As he conscientiously met my train.

Anna Louise ——————————————

MURDER STORY

He smiled and
held me there, I dried his eyes
wiped my soul with his passion
cake burning in the oven
nearly on fire
I was a cow
I don't know what he was
I was a slag
legs thrown over themselves
I cried, but only once.
He sang in the street and
boasted about me to his mates
I modelled myself
posed for pictures which tore
down my immune system.
I was good for nothing.
He had no money for electricity
I saved us
in the dark
voices called to me
and people talked
lice ran rampaging in my hair
I was a whore
drinking killed me
boasting hurt me
lorry drivers chatted me up
on the dry motorway
Icicles melted me
My hands are as rough now
as they were then.
Builders whistled at me,
my legs danced to moonlit tunes
hip-shaking insecurity blinded me.
I was good for nothing
cow, slag, whore, bitch.
He raped me
we threw condoms over
the floor like lost emotions
and grieved for our babies.

Wh**A**t will she think

If I mention the e**L**ectric shock treatment?

Casually plug **I**t

Into the conv**E**rsation?

How will she adjust her perceptio**N**s

The epilepsy w**A**s a challenge

(Had **T**o be confessed; I'm a non-driver).

So how w**I**ll she

Handle the fact that she's w**O**rking

Alo**N**gside a survivor?

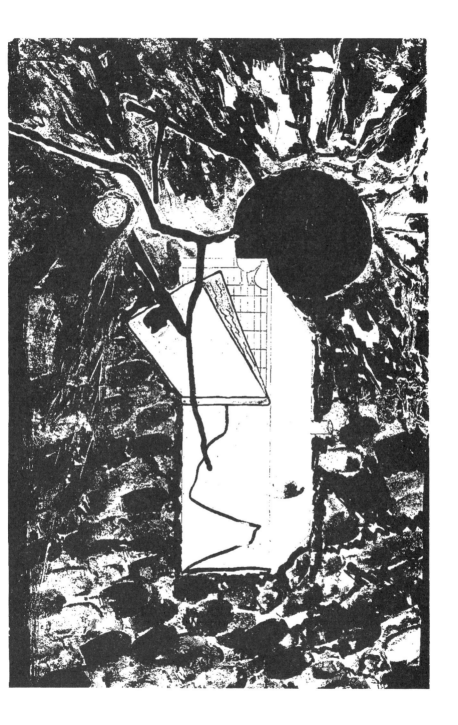

RAMPTON SPECIAL HOSPITAL

The sixth day

Is this a man?
Taller today – my nurse,
keeper of the keys.
Bigger, brighter,
they clang on his belt.

He happened to be born
on the right side
to a trade ready felled,
his union his ballast
keeping him true.

His granite fist
his pincer eyes
his chain lip
cut on the same lathe
passed grandfather, father, son.

He shovels me up
to limp to the blocked door.
Outside his village glints
beyond barbed walls
A long winter beckons.

Zeedy Thompson

TORMENTED REST

Doctors, psychiatrists, hospitals.
I must get out,
Depressing, humiliating.
"You'll never walk again"
Grim satisfaction;
My life's not worth living
I must be crazy
He says so, no . . . I'm not.

Unnecessary operation
Gives birth to tension.
Valium, pain killers
Give them up, take the lot
Stop them prodding
Asking stupid questions.
If only I could stop crying?
This drip is no consolation
The pain is shocking!

"Pull yourself together"
If a stern look could kill
I'd be gone,
My psychiatrist, bloody cynical man
He's not in pain . . .
I am, sod him . . .
I'm answering no more questions,

I'll stare into space, dumb,
Look at him
Biting his nails,
He should be lying here
Not me! now . . .
Pen poised in mid air
Inquiring about my family
They're my concern
Not yours, not anybodies.

Transferred at last,
To Orthopaedic hospital
Case file reads
"This woman is not insane
She complains of back-pain"
Six long months of tormented hell
Did not cast a dignified spell,
But at last someone listens
Who seems to care.

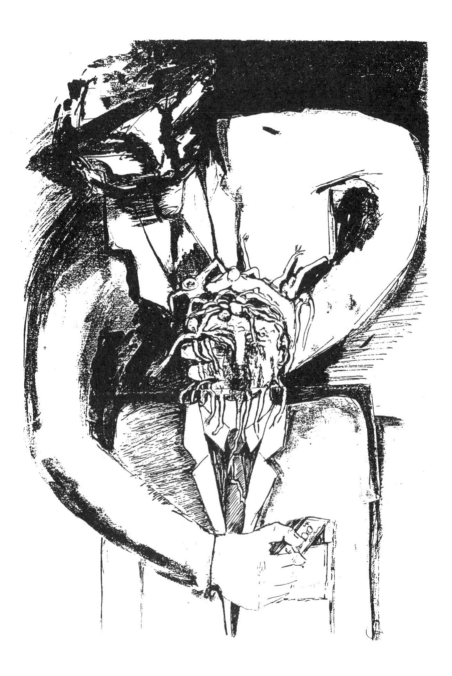

Maroushka Monro

EXCEPT FOR THE RECORD

On the analyst's couch
I've watched
talked
balked at questions
defiantly refused
to offer words of insight
fought the urge to get up and leave
grieving the loss of confidence
left hanging in the air
before being swallowed up
digested by the psychiatrist
for further analysis

I could not stand the burden
of holding onto my own truths –
in isolation they seemed
ruthless, invasive, unreal –
at first
revealing was a relief
a belief in sharing the impossible
beckoned like a recurring dream
the theme repetitious
haunting and familiar

but soon
the act of voicing my thoughts
enticed me to snatch them back
imagining if they were not verbalised
memorised
there would always be a doubt
of their existence
their persistence
might instead burn themselves out
shouting each other down
like a squawking family

even so
I chose to tell all to the analyst
while he listened sphinx-like
with acceptance
and no hint of emotion
mopping up my history
like a sponge
impinging on the spillage
for which he had no use
except for the record.

Wayne Tenyue

EVERY BADDY ARMY

Ah who dem
Ah who dem deh
Ah who dem
Ah who dem deh

With dem likle
roun shiel
With dem roun
iron head dress

Oh mussi Seasor
an him army
Prophecy did ah
wahn we
So prophecy
did ah tell we

Church man have dem army
Fire men have dem army
Police man have dem army
Soldier man have dem army

Post man is ah army
Doctor man have dem army
Pregnant woman is ah army
Picnie ha dem army

Black man ha no army
Black man ha no army
White man have no army
Multi racial army
Education army

Detention army
Old lady army
Like every baddy turn army
The whole world turn army
The whole world is ah army

Jeanette Ju-Pierre

MOTHER'S PAIN

Cupping my mother's pain of
50's doors
slamming back,
is bruising the delicate souls of people,
black, Caribbean smiles,
shrivelled up, huddled against
cold pavements, are paying their rent
through their flapping shoes!

The wearing of coloured shirts,
banana designs, waving promise of
freedom to communicate but wind-eaten by
winter winds blowing in the Archway
roundabout.

Laughing mouths stripped of mango-
eating feasts, cocoanut tree climbing and
the early morning dash to a silver-blue
sea as winter begins posing questions
about immigration laws.

Get to the back of the bus! yells somebody
taut and white. She faces a mask on a double
decker with words unspoken.

He is marching towards her in straight jacket blue.

A bird watches the exchange from his nest,
contemplating the black mother in no
man's land!

Bushy Kelly

EXTRACT FROM *LOSS*

Heart.
Soul.
Memory.
Remembrance.
Prayers.
Heart is beating.
Soul is reaching.
Memory is gone.
Remembrance is all.
Prayers are repeated again and again.
Art.
Family.
Community.
Story.
Death.
Art to escape the family and gain a community.
A story containing images of death speaking directly.
Reveal.
Hidden.
Public.
Trauma.
We need to face the violence
We need to face the murder.
We need to face the death.
We need to face the history.
We need to face the genocide.
We need to face the suicides of now and in the past.
Complete in itself words waft over our hearts and minds
speaking to the soul of experience,
of memory
of history.
Relaxed our voices mingle in sounds unspoken
but heard in the patterns of our body movements
the eyes wide in listening.

*(**Loss** is the third section of a trilogy and deals with multiple deaths amongst friends in 1992. This piece is dedicated to the Brixton Community Sanctuary.)*

REACHING THE MIDWAY MARK

reaching, for some reason, out for it
only to wake in a darkened room
where chair and clothes and bed

have no more weight than air has
in the daytime when all these things
are solid . . . mother, tell me.

Poet-mother, born of another
generation speaking through its own
veil, have you told me? I cannot find it.
Not the marrow, not the heart of it.
Is it

like daring to fill a room with light
when the house is dark . . .

how silence thins . . .
how sounds rush through in a sudden flood
but nothing breaks, not one thin strand
of silk ? Is it

like prising open a fruit to find
torn ligatures of strawberry ? Blue ,

a blue that goes with Egyptian gold,
the bluest of blues the minute before
night thins itself with morning ? Heavy ,

disembodied ? How the first time feels
when you ask a man *can I kiss you* , is it
how day and night change places ?
To do with articles of clothing ?
All the things I could tell you mother ?
All the things they tell me.

Alan Daffern

SUNDAY AT DANA'S

We talk for an hour
about adult things.
I help wrap
children's Christmas memories.
From the cold
the girls arrive,
muddy from the farm,
feeding puppies and geese.

Mom tells her youngest off;
She stands sensitive and shy.
"Your feet are dirty
  and your school collar black".
Remembering my
childhood pain I say
"You're embarrassing her
  in front of me".

She is at that "funny" age.
Not a child,
but neither a woman.
She fancies the boy
as I once fancied the girl.
Wishing she did not
wear glasses,
that an adult world
was not now settling
upon her shoulders.

Maybe it is the sadness
that still haunts me,
the missed chance
to be called daddy,
or simply knowing
how painful
childhood can be.

Val Stein

SYLVIA, THANKS A BUNCH

*I wrote this after reading the poems of Sylvia Plath
and continually encountering hideous disability imagery.
EG, describing trees blowing in the wind, she writes
"So the deaf and dumb/Signal the blind, and are ignored . . ."
Later, I came across the line "We touch like cripples . . ."*

We touch like cripples,
like conspirators,
like those who understand
each other's lives,
reaching past the old tracked scars
the world leaves
as it rolls heavy over us.

At times with daily clumsiness
fumbling against our bruised places,
at times awed blank
or stone uncaring
at the chasm of our differences;
sometimes with deliberation
carving new cliffs with malicious pick,
but sometimes launching ourselves freely
into the dividing air.

And we touch like cripples together,
leaning one against the other,
holding those who have gone
for all their lives unheld,
reaching out to those against whom
walls have bricked in each possibility,
to those whom others have touched
with knives,
with drugs,
with ECT.

We touch with tenderness,
with knowing,
tentatively,
sensually,
raucously,
with laughter,
with fear,
with strength.

Johnny Crescendo

MY BIRTHDAY SUIT

I have worn clothes.
I have had images.
I have surrounded myself with the fabric of design.
I have had change and voice and
I have dressed and undressed.
and, after having looked for the clothes that represent me,
I have ended up naked, in my birthday suit.

This offends people.
and, speaking for myself, I'm not quite comfortable . . . . .
yet.
I'm working on it.
I have faith because every time I put on an appliance
people make comments about my history,
of how they used to know me,
of how I used to be . . . .
one of the lads
for all that.

My birthday suit
is quite old and well worn.
It has grown with me and I have grown with it.
In the garbage of the garb
I pulled away in useless attempts to cover up
to sneak away like a spy for the other side.
Them!
But I have never really escaped, lied or tricked
anyone but myself.
Perhaps that's why we dress because the truth is,
for some,
unacceptable.

So here I am, naked, bare, starkers.
Alone with you and my pen.
Wondering what you need me to put on.
Wondering what I need to put on.
And where that need comes from.
And will I do it for you?

CLAIRE

My friend Claire
Descends the stair
With a delicate air
And a definite flair

With casual poise
She heeds not the noise
Of the rutting boys
And their smuttering ploys

Nor their marriaging peals
Nor the carriaging wheels
The clicking of heels
Or the jigging of reels

Nor whistles nor cheering
She toys with her ear-ring
Claire has no hearing
And Claire doesn't care.

Ferenc Aszmann ───────────────────

HEART UP A MOUNTAIN

They were carrying this bloody great heart up a 1-in-1 mountain
And they asked me to help.
"What's in it for me?" I yelled as I spun by en route for oblivion
"Well you won't get paid", they gasped a pushin.
"Well that suits me fine"

This mountain was surrounded by senseless realities,
        stinking in everrepetitive mediocrity.
It was from them I was trying to escape so up the mountain I go,
        yes or no
Well of crazy course I will I do.

The heart was bigger than all the people pushing it up put together.
When I got my arms stuck it got bigger still, everyone cursed
        cos it was heavier
Hated me for a moment then accepted me as a lifelong friend.

So infinity's just a jumped-up millimetre, it's a millisec to pretty eternity
And one day we'll look back on our own and all sentient suffering
As but a momentary blink of heaven's sublime perversity.
So all that misery we had and heard about didn't go on that
        long after all.
Oh the perils of negative vision – funny how real it all seems
        at the time, eh?

Yet here I am hopelessly carrying up a gigantic heart
Feelin inside like I'm being bathed in broken glass . . .

The air got scarcer, the sweat profuser
By nightfall I felt we'd have gotten nowhere
Til recall of day and night being identical, nevershifting sickly grey
And weather having ceased to exist for as long as anyone could say
And I hadn't felt anything for years, didn't know anyone who had
And I'd abandoned squirming for survival in a familiar cesspit.
For pushin a giant heart up a mountain with a bunch of strangers
I'd ceased to exist – that's the kindest you could say about me.

The first few centuries were unbearable, nobody spoke 'cept to recruit
And nobody looked at anybody and averted always were all our eyes.
It required some kind of co-operation, in unison blankly single-minded.
There were no leaders or characters and we must've made a few
        miles up sometime
But the chill stench of nightmares we were somehow escaping
        were forever just as close behind.

One thing kept me (and for all I know us) going was the heart
        we transported was definitely beating
I knew somehow, couldn't hear it or feel it, and though we
        were never rescued
I know someday the endless mountainside will never end
And we will never stand upon the summit and look down with
        relief and unspeakable satisfaction
For the world has ended and though life does not go on
. . . something . . . . imperceptibly continues to exist.

DEAR YOU

You should try to love you
A little more than you do.
Not the you trapped in the prison of bone
but the bit of you that exists in all others.
Called the Christ by christians
and the Buddha by buddhists.

Nature does not hate itself.
Babies are born as I write and white hot
Blossoms of stars grow outward.

Nature does not hate itself.
Not even when hunting and feeding off itself.
So why should you?
Drink deep the sacramental wine of
whirling galaxies and wild suns.
Sing songs with saints and scientists,
beneath the synagogue of the sky.
Love nature, and remember,
The nearest bit of nature to you is you.

MADINAH

I saw
Eyes bright and shining
A vital love and laughter
In the secrets of your smile
A hidden gleam
That blood red stream
Bursting from your soul

I saw
Tears upon tears
Welling from the deep
Resounding echoes
In the silence
Hugging at your heart
And a child
Grown old with grief
Force-fed misery
And pain

I saw
The harvest apples
Mannah from heaven
Ravaged windfalls
Free for all
Grown rotton on the ground

Well when you're ready
Rotting apples grow the richer
Make the sweetest cider
And I'll be sat beside you
While we drink to friendship
And nurse old wounds
Forever home !

A RADICAL IDEA

Here's a radical idea today,
Just show some respect for human beings.
What's to be gained by that old fashioned way
Of free market social engineering,
Do unto them as you do to yourself
I see what has been done to all of them
I don't here from you that same scream for help
Yes you! of that cosy think-tank system
What does your mother say, and who is she
Do your children beg for coins on the street.
Does where you live look like a catastrophe
Does your face have that grim look of defeat.
Show some respect, and see how rich life can be
All of us creating wealth, all as free.

Peter Campbell

THE MENTAL MARCHING BAND

You'd better wet your whistles
For the Mental Marching Band.
For we're making a wee comeback
And it's spreading through the land.
And we'd laugh you to distraction
If we thought you'd understand
About the Mental Marching Band.

There's Danny Ogenkenyu
On the bagpipes by the way.
And when he's took his Lithium
Sweet Jesus can he play.
You can denigrate the madness
The song won't fade away
From the Mental Marching Band.

We'll all be out and running
When the storm breaks.
Down the House of Commons
Wi' our fruitcake.
You'll have to take your medicine then
Just for the music's sake
And the Mental Marching Band.

We'll not be taking prisoners
Under blood red skies.
We've had too much confinement
In our own lives.
We're getting our own World War out
That everyone survives.
Thanks to the Mental Marching Band.
Let's hear it.

David Kessel

MIKE MOSELY

there is a conspiracy against
the social-democracy of the
British common people.

Grey, calloused, forgotten at fifty
he has given his all; his wiry heart,
his skilled, locked fingers, his
chipped backbone, his broken welding
language, for this choking fag,
this dark, blinding pint
this scouring Irish lament.

Scorned, down for a bundle in bird,
forsaken by wives and the DSS,
shy of nothing 'cept himself,
to this bare room, phlegm and
loneliness between the stubborn
slums and the useless sirens.

Driven by fury to this back ward,
wasted, ulcered, unforgiving.

– start from here to make anew
the happiness of children playing
beneath heeding, enduring gulls
in a wooded, tempered land.

STIGMA

The real mark, the one that doesn't fade
is not what people think or say,
but the stain inside
the sick cell in the bone,
the constant damaging thought
that this machine is faulty
this thinking can't be trusted.

If you were a cynical social manipulator
what better weapon?
The flowering cancer seed of doubt
will stop more rebellious acts
than a thousand police with riot shields.

SOCIAL SERVICES TISSUES

I have been in two of the
Counselling Rooms
now.
both have two uneasy chairs
and a low "coffee" table
although we always drink tea.

on the table in each room
is a cheap aluminium ashtray
– weightless –
for the security of staff
I presume, on my second visit
when I am a little more able to take in
my surroundings.

and a box of tissues.

I had thought they would hide these –
have them in a drawer
to pull forth
like a string of bright magician's handkerchiefs
when a CRISIS loomed
but no, they sit there
waiting
expecting.

the expectation of the whole place
is that people will want to be miserable here.
by my fourth visit this has got to me
– I want to arrive in bowler hat, tails and a cane
and clatter-tap my way
across the gloomy Social Services hallway
and up the badly carpeted stairs
singing some crass musical number.

COMMUNITY

There's "Can't in the Community",
There's "Critical of me in the Community",
There's "Cruel in the Community"
There's them that are ignoring me,
There's even some avoiding me,
There's crying but not heeding me,
There's words that cannot access me,
There's only half the therapy.
There's nobody available.

There's homelessness where one's told to be,
"Bloody working you lazy git," but
There's no job for me and that was the first casualty.
There's "Equality" but that doesn't apply to "Disability".
There's Friendship and there's Family –
But I mustn't tell the Family,
And the friends are "Mental" same as me –
The hospital's our Community,
And they're closing the community.

There's a "Chemical Straightjacket"
That means that we,
Sit silently, lonely, passively,
Needing someone to talk to me,
But what "Care in the Community."

DON'T TOUCH

"Don't touch!" they cried
They really meant no harm, had not intended
To make a shaking apoplectic
With their nagging.

"Don't touch!" for their interior decor
Indeed was fragile and expensive,
Themselves and furniture alike
To them untouchable, those self-pariahs.

There are no easy stages;
Somebody's lost a memory,
Somebody's taking shocks;
The papers are in order.

Don't touch, then you'll keep out of trouble;.
Don't lead, don't show,
Just pump and load.

You're only sure you're sane, okay,
When one like you is locked away.

There rooted the bare, threaded nerve,
The stunted limb, enfeebled grasp, the shake.

"Don't touch!"
Their errors paralyse them.

He only wanted to make something work;
"Don't touch; he might be dead."

Debbie McNamara ———————————

LIFE *(caught short abroad)*

There are three wards in the women's compound
Bound by a twenty-foot wall
Broken by a huge wooden gate
With a padlock like that
Where twenty-four hours a day
A uniformed guard sits, lies or sleeps
Safely on the other side
Immune to the ceaseless begs and pleas
From the despairing ones inside.

There are two round holes cut into the prison gate
Not for the good of any in here,
But so the scared-looking jailor
Can check there are no potential escapees
Loitering with too-obvious intent
When he quickly unwraps the chains of their suffering,
Tantalises with a glimpse of freedom
Snatched just as quickly away
At staff hand-over time,
Leaving us all salivating and hungry
Three times a day.

Sometimes men come to the gate
To stand and stare
Into the inner sanctum
Where the women are reminded of their
Single, short, asylum issue gown
Which mocks at the dignity of a sari,
And they melt into invisibility
With their eyes downcast for shame

A few are driven by need and by panic
To scream for rupees, chai, a bidi.
Eyes fixed ahead, faces like deathmasks,
Hair shaved short in case of lice –
Hollow-eyed souls hanging on at any price.

And I don't know when I am leaving
My friends can't reach me now
When I look at the faces around me
I see what they do to you here.
So I'm hanging on at any price
Trying to keep – temperate.
The monsoon is about to break;
I think, and wait, and sweat.

Mike Lawson ————————————————————

COMMUNITY CARE ON BENEFITS

Antipsychotic medication used to hibernate livestock
and stain microscopic slides is what they call the stuff that takes too many lives.

Psychotherapy is the arrogance of someone who assumes they can guide your life

Makes you wonder who is crazy, is it them or us?
The shrink takes the taxi, we live on a 'bus
It is in the mind of the beholder; the one with the keys
All about power and imaginary disease.

Get your brains blown out for your own good
The psychologist looks at me as if I am wood
Show me the inkblots I'll tell you no lies
Some shrink got admitted – he thinks he can fly, which
is more reasonable than believing in schizophrenia
They never called him crazy for that but now they do
Dopamine and Serotonin messed up with chemicals
We sometimes make snowballs with our dreams and weave them in the day room
waiting for night and a little sodium amytal somnambulation
Social control with an angry nurse wanting to push the button
We walk through virgin snow to get shocked by E.C.T.
It is the most elaborate expensive way to get sweet tea
The whole thing takes the biscuit at the price
of personal dignity
We are not axe murderers who are lazy the stuff makes us hazy
Unable to rhyme in a dissonant *worl–d* running out of time
Lunatic psychiatrists continue to bake a psychiatric souffle
We recipients and survivors are the scapegoats
Of multinational pharmaceutical profit making
If only the shrink and his apologists could understand
That they cannot stop the music of the mental health marching band.

Paul Mathew ────────────────

A DATE WITH THE MEDICAL MODEL

He's a hard-nosed quack
With a cheap wise-crack
His professional smile
Hides a hooker's guile
He'll give what he needs
But more fun if you plead
Want a quick striptease?
On your knees!
He'll flash expertise
A little Latin and Greek
Scientific mystique
All the tricks of the trade
Until you're laid
On his couch.

Practice safe sex in that
Cosy sess with the shrink
(Barrier methods are best)
Don't get too close
Or you'll get a dose
Of moralistic clap –
Trap – no way out
Whatever you do
He'll label you
And no intercourse
Is not a safe bet
Silence won't make it easier
You'll be odds-on fave for
Paranoid schizophrenia
So you're fucked if you talk
Fucked if you don't
His view is the same
But the treatment's different
Cause he'll attach blame
To struggle
You're punished for fighting
And wanting to choose
Praised for passivity
In the face of abuse.

So if you're exhausted
By the bump and the grind
If you're disheartened
When the sparks start to fly
Relax – the doctor's your friend
And for him you'll be patient
Till the bitter
End.

Francis Bangay

A JOURNEY THROUGH
THE PSYCHIATRIC CORRIDORS

They label themselves as normal
They label us as mad
But the effect of this ideology
Becomes a little sad,
So many of us get lost
So many of us get forgotten
The soul struggles against so many years of assault.

This is the road we wander up and down
This is the road we cadge cigarettes on.

They label themselves as normal
They label us as mad,
But our anger is our assertiveness
Not an illness we should apologise for,
Feet shuffle on hospital lino
Open mouths
Staring eyes
And institutionalised clothes
For years we have been suppressed by psychiatric drugs.

This is the road we wander up and down
This is the road we cadge cigarettes on.

They label themselves as normal
They label us as mad
So often they speak on our behalf
But so many stories need to be told
So we become the scapegoat of many comedians jokes
But we don't need this scorn
As we get lost in a psychiatric ghetto
Always seen as the problem
But right now we're looking for our voice.

This is the road we wander up and down
This is the road we cadge cigarettes on.

They label themselves
They label us too
And the do-gooders run their nice little charities
And the scientists dither about
Looking for that elusive gene

But I think they fumble in the dark
So many myths can be seen through
Once you know
And now you know
The rhythm of the spirit will be proud and strong.

Where is the road we seek freedom on?
Where is the road we find our liberation on?

Outside the Psychiatric Institution

This Lonely Places

OLD AGE

Age slips in unnoticed
Like the sly tide
In its erosion.

People rush to offer seats in buses.
First one laughs defensively, ignoring time's disguise.
Then, disheartened, one accepts.

When people see an old woman
Stare too long in the glass,
They thing she is vain.

They do not know
With what anguish she sees her face,
and wonders at its new born ugliness,
Then laughs, in order not to weep.

Fatma Durmush

FATHER'S RAGE

We came to greet you, oh father.
Where are you now, father?
Rages have boiled you down,
made a skeleton of you. Now
we are sitting down
in the cosy chairs of despair.

As you battle it out between your dual selves,
your face expressionless,
as another cell in your brain dies.
Old age is creeping in, and you'll
die – altogether.

Where did you find all the good news?
you ask, again with no expression,
your hair all gone and your mouth
frothing. Mother is sitting in the easychair.
She is crying.

"I've had enough
 of beatings. Old man,
 sit by me so that we
 can die in peace."

Why did you do it, oh father?
Mother and I are powerless.
There's no end to our suffering.

Mother and you are old.
We children of your blood
await your getting better.
In vain. You are a happy man
in your despair.

Another year passes,
another century's coming.
Soon I'll find
nothing but bad about you.
I'll go abroad.

Bill Capwell

MONSOON, I'M ALONE

Monsoon
Rush of air
Sheets of rain
Can't see through
Paddies pregnant in erotic desire
Dalliers green grey haze
Mud turned into red paste
Totally wet drowning in despair
Cigarettes decadence to nothing
No light
No fire, but wet blizzard
Shaken cold death
Clinging to one another for warmth
Walking dance of death in neon light
Rain drops echo on leaves
Sea gentle waves/music to shore
Darkness of morning
Seagoddess rising with rain and surf
Child playing in puddles
Mother's caring
Change your wet clothes, there's none
Monsoon in mind, past and present
Clash at the door, I'm alone.

David Russell ─────────────

INTELLECTUAL'S RELATIONSHIP SONG

I never go to gypsies to find out about my fortune,
I have cast off superstitions of the past;
I am a product of an era of built-in obsolescence
Where relationships are just not made to last.

My world is morning grey; I have learned to live with it,
That's a promise that to myself I vowed;
Because I've been set free by clinical psychiatry
And no facile solutions are allowed.

The highways of your mind are quite forbidden to pedestrians,
That's tough on me, I'm trying to be naïve;
For when it comes to making statements
From the bedrock of my feelings,
It's the tongue inside my cheek I must believe.

You see, I read you up in books before I ever saw your face,
And now it's just your ambiguities I see,
And as I wander
Through those labyrinthine depths of inner meanings
I think the only one I'm talking to is **me**.

I thought my being lonesome might place me on a pedestal
But now I see I'm in a lonely crowd
Of people all set free by clinical psychiatry
And no facile solutions are allowed.

We're half-past liberation,
Nothing's right and nothing's wrong;
There's just a big complex of different points of view;
And my vast array of paperbacks
Has so broadened my outlook
That I make all the allowances for you.

Yet you still seem to be present
As a sensory phenomenon
And this poor superego can't be proud,
Because I've been set free by clinical psychiatry
And no facile solutions are allowed.

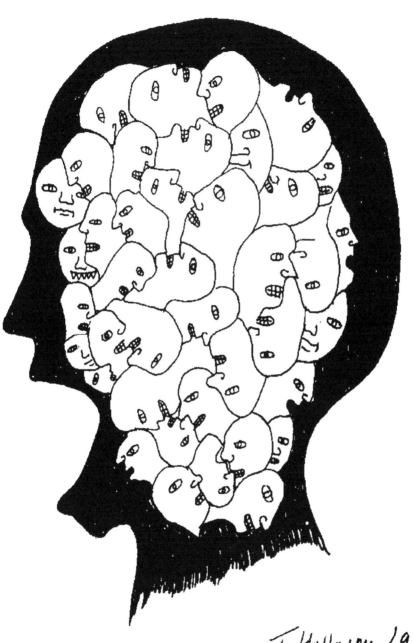

J Holloway '94.

THE GREENMAN

Break
through
this petrified logic.
Speak of the
bio-degradable art
of the forest floor,
where matter breaks down,
where life is recycled
in mould and mulch.
Neither the vanity of kings and bishops,
of theologians and politicians
could hold you
in its stone straightjacket.
You are what cannot be contained.
Our minds are cathedrals
dreaming they are forests.
Our stone faces crack,
we are coshed by chemicals,
fastened by fashions and therapies.
But just as old leaves
are turned into new forests,
every breakdown, in its green alchemy,
if recognised,
should
be a
break
through

Michael Horovitz

COMPOSED UPON WESTMINSTER BRIDGE, 1993
(Homage to Wordsworth)

Earth has but little air to breathe
Or greenery to share; battalions of the homeless wear
Their sleeping bags and boxes like a prayer,
But cast-off newsprint's the best they're like to thieve
From this heartless business efficiency display.
Smoke from mighty vehicle exhaust
And cancer snort clogs every ray
Of sun that percolates the coarse
Polluted surface of concrete-shadowed river:
Dear Christ! this filthy water's
Thick enough to walk on – but all trace of laughter's
Quickly spent, as another bomb scare gets the cops a-quiver.
Wordsworth, thou shouldst be living at this hour
In parliament, to put your grass-roots dawn back into power.

Danielle Hope

THE COUNTRY OF STELAZINE

Today you played snakes and ladders
to keep quiet and ignore
the nurses in their glass tower
or the boy who strokes ping-pong balls
as if each was a magic lamp.
You've been told that this is a hospital
but you know: this is the country
of Stelazine – a blue pill
that comes flickering and fidgeting
out of your fingers and feet

A small blue pill, just like the button
you once lost from your favourite party dress.
Your mother squeezing your wrist
as she tapped a vast door –
"Remember to say please and thank you".
How you played snakes and ladders then.
Small fists pushed counters over
an endless board. How you fought
but rarely won.

From a room smelling of iodine
a doctor comes, pastry chef proud,
bearing the diagnosis
they've been baking for weeks.
Agitated para-schizophrenia.
Yes, you had yelled:
"Get away you buggers, damn it!"
And cut yourself free at the wrist.
Her heels click away like loose teeth.
You toss the dice, slip down a snake.

The snake we all have waiting, with a label
and a pale blue pill in its mouth.

Jade Reidy

SELF-RELIANCE

If the sky rained answers
I wouldn't mind getting wet
if the earth erupted solutions
I'd live under a volcano
if the sea washed waves
of explanations to the shore
I'd be a beach bum
if the wind with its sweeping
gestures unravelled riddles
I'd be a kite caught up in its breath
if the fire offered salvation
would I jump into it?

You know how it is
you go along awhile thinking
"Well, if this is life
I can handle it nicely thanks"
and the very next day
the whole ceiling falls
in on your head
and there's nowhere
to turn but
inwards

Aaron Williamson————————————————

EXTRACT FROM *A HOLYTHROAT SYMPOSIUM*

Cunctation of the adage, a wiper face: consult the next
page; it spits as you lift it

matriculation ticktacked, a swampum, some sump herein

octaves emitting a mould of breath, clung down as forge-cack:
a handle and

bevelled into entera

beginning at the kind of gleam that's always under the block

its bridle, extrusioned as abutment

shoulderblades, dentures, other clausatives

a visceral fixture: do not give it your notice

No teeth! No other residency but in the pressurised fluvia

adjoining hot tongs, calefacient and loading

a peninsula, an architectural swivelling

cross-bred between expectorations, the found slot

hawking the centrifuge

centripetal cusp

intransitive from having kindred in its groin

scratching and tracing iridescent synergies

this locus is nibbling a fritterment of cadence

*(A Holythroat Symposium is a collection of poetry and prose by
Aaron Williamson, who is profoundly deaf.)*

Yvonne Houlton

EVIL

Gash! Her smile rips canvasses! A red slip of muscle.
Divinely finding some intellect to hold onto, like a bone.
Heralding the archetype. Sex slides along its bannisters.
Wool woofs.
A horny creation slides its bottom along a tarmacked road.
The leash tightens.
Then pain, like love.
A jam sandwich in white bread, eaten whilst the egg and
spoon race
frightens us.

A MAN'S WORLD

The white snow
greets the black earth

Rivulets of fire
needle the earth's cloth

Man's torso
fits his waist

Women's breasts
socket in

A slice of day,
a spread of night

Grey voices
echo in a garage

A limousine
slides its coins along the road

A sixties beehive
blows bubbles with bees in

A shattered glass
held together by a spider's web

Old wallpaper
flakes with milk

A lorry
in love with an ant

New York ageing

Diamond corners. Cars. A man swirled

Cut out an instant

Michael Horovitz

SAME OLD-WORLD-DISORDER BLUES

    ... Dull opiates, the technological millennium, famine
All continuing, thriving — with terrorists, pseudo-religious
Fixers and hucksters in vogue, inter-
Nationalist gang wars, unbreakable cupidinous
Chains of death sentence: State eats State, Superstar
Complete Unknown, punks scream for more and beat
Each others' heads in — unaware
Of real wild life and vegetation
Dumb to scream *their* outrage   ... of literature
Reduced to counter-denunciations, party lines
Conveyor-belts, trade counters. Wised up
Students need their good
Grades, for who survives in the west without self-
Promotion —   Then what society
Is this, predatory jungle, spurning the basis
Of its self-possession — that soldiers and idealists
Fought together, worked apart, under-
Wrote a withdrawal from killing? Yet what else gives now
But a slower demoralising of each neighbour, each
'Friend', if they venture on the other's pitch – what use
Writing for sale, when to be read
For what one is worth
Means the reader gives up buying
The sales conference vision
— *Ever bigger profits* — without which
The untouchable bankruptcy
Of the dead-end process
Pushes
      the pusher
          off the edge
Of the corporation's top
Penthouse balcony
To lie immobile, redundant — peace at last
Alongside the dissolving
Wrappers of The Product
On the pavement –
Splayed out, gutter
Of Babylon.

David Russell

ECO THUNDERSTORM

You turn on the gas, you squirt the sprays
Make a haze of expectancy,
Your every breath can tip all the scales
And uproot every tree.

You can lace the rains and breed the algae,
Scum up every shore,
You can set the barometer of all mankind
Wobbling forever more.

You tossed me up, you bounced me down,
Batted me like a whingeing child;
With your magic, winding, twisting dance
You can drive any statue wild.

You can blow me up to old King Kong
You can shrink me to Tom Thumb;
You can blank the light of a million stars
Strike all politicians dumb.

You're the greenhouse effect we can't reject,
You strip the ozone layer,
You can break all the banks, make the old Thames flood,
Answer every devil's prayer.

I thought my sanity was sunk
In a pile of solid rock;
But you're an aerial earthquake, undermining,
Running all the world amok.

> *You turn us to a hundred celsius*
> *Though you think yourself luke-warm;*
> *You're the end of every element —*
> *You're the Eco Thunderstorm.*
>
> *You are the alpha, the omega ray,*
> *Turning every night to a scorching day.*

Dinah Livingstone —————

AUGUST IN LEICESTER SQUARE

Heat eats energy
snaffles soul.
Your will to work
falters to a halt.
You are stuck.

Everyone you know has gone
from this desert,
London shut shop
conversation dried up
streams dust defeated.

But with early evening
all the way from Piccadilly
to Leicester Square
down to St Martins in the Fields –
where are stooks and harvest mice? –

up past Cambridge Circus
yes less miserable
there is an amazing
honeysweet beehive hum
a clogged buzzing.

I am suddenly aware: it's people talking
but mostly foreign languages. This year
I can't even tell what they are
and no one talks to me.
I am the alien.

Empty without input
I take a tip from all these voices
on a trip from their home fields or cities:
Time to summer off out.

7.30 STREETS OF LONDON

Coming out the tube at Leicester Square
A busker tunes his guitar
People rush around avoiding the cars
The taxis, the buses, the pain
Of other people . . . . . .

We're all here to be entertained
Piccadilly lights flash on and off
The buildings shake their shadows
Fat pigeons glide above the kamikaze traffic . . .

We loon around
Kiss one another
On the creaking escalator
Entertainment enough
Amidst the hard-sell of this universe

The stars are invisible
Excitement cranks up the nerves
Of the city

A tramp begs coins
Like a desperate friend.

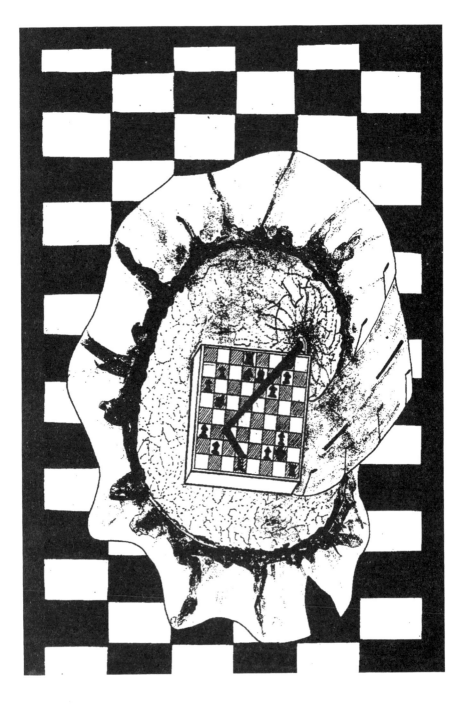

Justin Quail

ASYLUM

The syringe of dreamy nothingness
hits the flesh, in another part of the
hospital a game of chess;
the patient recuperates, pulls up
his trousers on the ward.
He has fallen overboard where the white rover
has suffocated him into laxity,
cancelled his debt of propriety
and has flung him into a dream,
with his program of the week in his pocket,
he takes a guess, passes the people
playing chess down the white corridor,
past doors and notice boards,
to avoid the system with its flaws,
open the dormitory door down more corridors
to the white zone, where he finds himself alone.

CHORUS FROM THE CLINIC

Somewhere we are numbers
lurking in the deeps
of a computer

Somewhere by our numbers
we have diseases, doctors seen
and drugs.

Somewhere by our diseases,
we have little pound signs,
pluses and minuses.

Somewhere by our pound signs
there is counted costs
and billing.

And somewhere there is someone
opening the bills,
with our numbers,
our diseases, doctors, drugs,
our pound signs,
our pluses, our minuses.
Again adding up the numbers,
and checking whether
we are dead.

Peter Street ─────────────

INSTITUTIONALISED

Exhausted Chrysanths drip down
twisted vases
flooding the formica table.

While our minds walk in the shade
we dip our toes in the sunshine
tasting happiness.

And place bets on the depths of seas
lashed against chrome lighthouses:
salt and pepper pots.
Until nurse parts the waves
with her handbrush.

Lunch-time, we enjoy; the same faces,
same meat, two veg, and a puddin'.

Plates cleared, we spend
the rest of the clock on memories.

Peter Campbell

NOT TO DIE, THANK YOU

They are trying not to die
On Villiers Street.
On John Adam Street
Beside the steps
That lead up to the Strand
They are living off glances
Loose gestures from smart handbag queens
And merchants of the quick dip.

On Hungerford Bridge
(The sixteenth favourite view
Of London)
There are two of them in place.
One at each end.
Folded up into the railings
Squatting
To be down there
And not take up
Too much of the walking space.

Congruous
As eels on a tin plate
They have curled themselves
Into our thumbs.
Yes – and we don't belong here.
Yes – but we're not gone yet.

Visits to Box Hill
On Sundays
Will not cure us of this.
Watching the leaves turn brown
Feeling the structure of the earth.
This is another form of dying.
One that we balloted for
And can't be rubbed out
By a tightening of the groin.

This is a different touch.
A gentle
Relentless stubbing
Of the big toe into the soft.

They are trying not to die on Villiers Street.
We disembowel ourselves
Rather too quietly.

Anna Neeter ─────────────────────

NEW YEAR IN THE ASYLUM

This could and should be such a healing place.
Even in Winter-time stirrings of Spring
Pulse all around, whisper among the boughs
Of trees fit for the parklands of a king.

The great, majestic forms rise from green swards
In rich array through avenue and glade
Where foxes unperturbed their prey pursue;
Gnarled roots hide homes by vole and hedgehog made.

Black birds and squirrels dart among the leaves;
Robins observe frail humans come and go,
From vantage points on walls and hedgerows where
Gold jasmine shines and scarlet berries glow.

Tall windows in the walls of mellowed brick
Look upon view to soothe the troubled gaze:
Soft, sweeping lawns by sheltered, winding paths
To wide horizons bathed in dreamlike haze.

Nature repairs the ravages of time
With green shoots on felled trunks; our man-made scars
Covers with verdant moss and russet leaves;
Transforms the jagged wires with frosty stars.

And yet within nothing but tinsel shines
No pictures painted here adorn the walls,
Though for the artist, space and light abound
And to the poet pain and beauty call.

All that once calmed the refuge-seeking soul
Is lost in toxic treatments of our time;
Greenhouse and kitchen gardens a disgrace;
People now ashen-faced stand mute in line.

Few venture out, of seasons see scant change;
Man takes not nature's cue, nor seeks her grace,
The magic bullets dim the inmates' eyes,
Dull pain and joy, slow down once eager pace.

Shame on the pedlars of insidious death
Who steal the joy of each new precious day
From those who meet my call, "Happy New Year!"
With a grim stare, before they drift away.

Terry Simpson

CARELESSNESS IN THE COMMUNITY

I've tasted caramel in community ice-creams,
   heard carols and felt caresses,
   seen carats on gold rings
   and carapaces on tortoises.
I've ordered carafes in community wine-bars,
   and flinched at carcasses hanging in the butchers.
   there's cartels running things
   and cart-horses pulling things,
but it seems
      there's something
           missing.

There's carbon monoxide galore in the community,
   coming from cars with caravans,
   and I hear that carcinogens are amassing,
   and carcinomas are rapidly growing,
   (not to mention carbuncles).
There's caries in the teeth
   and carnage on the roads,
   Carmelites in retreats,
   and a few caribou in the Alaskan community,
but still
      there's something
           you don't much hear about.

I've heard of careers being made in the community,
   and carp in the pools,
   and caricatures making fools of people.
There's carnivals and carnivores,
   and carrots in fields
   and carob in the health shops,
   Cartesian philosophy,
   (at least I think there is).
There's carriages and carrion,
   and carabinieri in the Italian community.
There's cartridges shooting things down
   and caryatids holding things up,
but the thing
      I'd like to see
           is hard to find.

Char March

LEARNING THE ROPES

I sit huddled
and sobbing
on the thick hearth rug in
The Quiet Room.
this makes me feel
incredibly secure.
it's exactly the sort of thing
loonies do.
I'm not proving at all good
at being "normal",
failure pretty much all round,
but I'm learning the ropes here
quickly.
last week I caught myself rocking
backwards and forwards
in my chair,
moaning,
just like a real nutter.

Martin Henderson

THE SANCTUARY IN NORTH LONDON

Walter Cranmer, always available
Opens the door,
He owns this place
And has made it a refuge,
Those who come here are here,
Ostensibly
For cups of tea.
There are many refugees
From psychiatry, recent policies,
And conversation ranges widely –
Shabbiness reigns
Yet there are few enough
Places like this
In this time of "community care".

I meet here a woman
(Currently in hospital)
Fragile, illogical, sweet
A tender annual running to seed.
The muscular self-reliant
Stay for weeks.
The radio is always on,
Playing classical music.

There is a sense of caring
Rare except in hospital,
Perhaps at war.

People can relax, talk here
In this queer setting I unwind
Myself and leave
Happier than I came.

Paul Gerhard

LITTLE WILLIE, DOWN IN PECKHAM?

Little Willie's nurse, Fiona, told the news:
(Will it leave him in dreadful stews?)
That Sectorisation has come up, Willie is her man
About to be kicked out of Maudsley Hospital to Peckham.

She asked him to come up with a label
To stick into his sectorisation. He did dribble,
"*Sects In Peckham.*" She thought, "Mother!"
Saying, "*Sex in Peckham*? Give over."

Then he suggested, "*Down In Peckham.*"
She thought it had suburban glam,
She smiled and put it to her group:
Terry forecasted, "*Down and out in Peckham. In the soup*"

So Willie's Peckhamness begins. His hunger
Soon finds out there is no such dinner
As something for nothing in the community.
So he sneaks off, praying for impunity,

Back to the hospital. But it is quite demolished!
He is in a stew! He could have polished
It off with his sweat for sauce,
After all, Willie, now, is his own boss.

Little Willie loses his benefit – a morsel of a purse.
Does it go in Peckham's one armed bandit's curse?
Or do DHSS take all the credit
With their taking the mickey handfuls induced to debit?

He only asks at Peckham's Job Centre,
"Is their vacancy for a program seller
At a future coronation?" But he turns down the call
To sweep up horse muck at the next state funeral.

Little Willie is stuck with sectorisation.
It makes him go to the railway station –
To jump in front of a train!
On the day train drivers are on strike. The pain.

But Little Willie is as diverse
As the gravy train can nurse –
To let a psychiatric client stock
In the worst capable trap that hits the block

Of housing the wrong spirit
In: "Heavens! Nothing is never quite done without spirit!"

David Harley

GLASS

. . . between me
in my personal space
and you
safe and alert at the nurse's station amid
glass
worked into medicine bottles
                    specimen bottles
                    hypodermic barrels

glass
protects the fire alarm
and you, the fireman

glass
litters the floor
where a tantrum exploded

Outside peers nervously between metal bars
protecting

glass

and you from me
and me from you
or me

mostly
this locked ward resembles
a glass case
or a cage of mirrors

Billy Childish

THE POETRY RACKET
(den Haag 93)

reading amongst the last generation now
boys from the liverpool scene
grey beards
sad little pony tails
and bald heads

we are introduced and stand chatting
by the book stall
there is nothing to say
and much rubbing of eyes
and thank fuck they dont name drop
these contemporys of lennon and mccartney

i stand nodding
and whatch my mouth
hardly a youth myself now
but still up for a fight
still biteing

but id be wasting my time hateing
these dear old boys
they have nothing left to say
theyre merely eeking out a living
doing the circuit
the schools
the radio
the odd telly voice-over
the poetry racket

surviving you could say
mean of mouth
with nothing bad to say about anyone

(Billy Childish is dyslexic; this poem appears as written by the author.)

Brian Docherty————————————————

GOT THEM MARTIAN DELTA BLUES AGAIN

Today's radio mixes music and memorials
twenty years ago Hendrix crashlanded
skip search/ memory bank/ Summer '67

Top of the Pops darkens my father's face
trying to decode the Hendrix drawl
was that "Kiss the sky" or "Kiss this guy" ?

Either way I don't care that's my song
flashback / first hearing / Cream's *I Feel Free*
stranger change than puberty done without drugs

Family jokes about changelings make sense
if I sprouted antennae and turned green
it couldn't match the brain chemistry

Now *Purple Haze* charges the breakfast air
as I eat my mushroom omelette with ginseng tea
shaping up to do the weekend shopping

Strolling round Spaceship Sainsbury's
seems sort of . . . . different somehow
even the uniforms are brighter and tighter

"Good Morning, this is Captain James T. Kirk
welcome aboard the 10am service to Mars
we hope you have a pleasant trip . . . .

Lights flash and tremble vibration rises
uniforms surround me "Walk this way Sir
stowing away is a VERY SERIOUS OFFENCE"

OhshitI'msoconfused / I LOVE YOU Lt. UHURA
it's all a game for robots in suits
the invaders from the Planet Grocer

*Seenyoursort . . . manytimes . . . affront . . . decentsociety
. . . business . . . protected . . . commonthieves . . .
suitabledeterrent . . . reports . . . Planet Broadmoor . . .*

Paul Gerhard

DALI

Dali paints Gala undraped, bar a
garland, with a blood red rose to the fore,
around her swallow neck.
Stalin winks on a badge he wears.

> Dali doubts God's infinitude and says,
> "God is not aware of the existence of Coca-Cola
> or of Salvador Dali, much less
> something called mortals."
> (Like a nineteen-sixties top-pop
> Botticelli billionaire
> without too much psychedelia?)

'My astute vicar says,
"They're not content with one world
to lump the poor into.
No, they need two worlds
to lump the poor into.
And Coca-Cola costs – money's what
they haven't got enough of in the Third World.
If you give the Third World money,
all they'll do is buy arms
(no, not arms for the poor)
and base narcotics.
God help us all if we give
the Third World money!"'

> Dali paints the bottom of
> 'Christ of St John of the Cross'
> like "I'm from Figueras,
> and Jesus' lovers
> that's my own open boat
> withdrawn from the waters onto the bank.
> Gala's and my bank.
> No, not the one we left empty-handed!
> The peseta appeal. (Where did my last million go?)
> Gala, she's my lady
> posing nude in lots of my pictures.
> This time I've got Jesus
> stuck upon the cross
> staring down
> despondently at my own personal heaven,
> doing his topless stint."

(Me, virgin on the absurd,
  wanking over Madonna, thinking "You Only Live Twice!")

Ricardo Corvalan

LIMP

(Angola at the present time has 50,000 amputees due to the mines supplied to the UNITA rebels by Britain, the USA and the former South Africa.)

I
As a
Chilean
Developed a
  Limp

The
British
Were kind
They
Gave me a
  Stick

I
As an
Angolan
Developed a
  Stump

The
British
Were kind
They
Planted the
  Mine . . .

I
As the
Minister
Said
NO!
To the child

Crutches
And sticks
Cost plenty
Of money

(But
The minister
Is kind)

Give the
Angolan
Three
Inches of
  Mine!

David Kessel

IRELAND

In a Kerry bus station jackdaws eat rubbish
An old republican carries plastic bags
Weighted with friendship and old ham.
The hills bequeath the memories of the troubles
And a longing for young bloodied boots. Great
Age has made this land schizophrenic, with
Deidre's love and Kilkenny races; suffering
Suffering in old faithful faces, and affluent contempt.

The cars run on slaughtered pigs. A man
Who carried a gun now has a hacking cough.
On bended knees this land lives, hard
Slog and the crack at street corners.
A whistled song and the jackdaw soaring
Over misogyny and open serious faces.

ACKNOWLEDGEMENTS

SURVIVORS' PRESS thanks each of the contributors for texts or illustrations published in this anthology for the first time.

For permission to publish text which is copyright material, we gratefully acknowledge the following:

Psychopoetica (Vol. 14, Spring 1989) for *Acting Like a Madman* by Nicky Stones.

The Road to Our Awakenings (CAPO, 1990) for *A Journey Through the Psychiatric Corridors* by Francis Bangay.

Matter of Life and Death (Zzero Books 1990) for *Coward* by Joe Bidder.

The Popular Front of Contemporary Poetry (Apples & Snakes 1992) for *These Days . . .* by Pitika Ntuli.

Grandchildren of Albion (New Departures 1992) for *I Used to be a Girl* by Ifigenija Zagoricnik-Simonivic.

Bricolage (Hangman Records 1992) for *Intellectual's Relationship Song* and *Eco Thunderstorm* by David Russell.

A Holythroat Symposium (Creation Press 1993) for *An Extract* by Aaron Williamson.

Disability Arts Magazine (1993) for *Don't Touch!* by David Russell.

Asylum (Spring 1993) for *Community* by Carole Batton.

BOADICEA (GLAD 1993) for *Sylvia, Thanks a Bunch* by Val Stein.

Amphora for Metaphors (Gnostic Press & Diamond Press 1993) for *AJ* by Richard McKane.

Flight of the Shaman (Paradigm Shift 1993) for *Flight of the Shaman* by Bill Lewis.

Out of the Fire (Spike Books 1993) for *Institutionalised* & *Leaving Hospital* by Peter Street.

Second Sight (Katabasis 1993) for *August in Leicester Square* by Dinah Livingstone.

Crushed Calabash (Hearing Eye 1994) for *Mother's Pain* & *Totanka Tatanka* by Jeanette Ju-Pierre.

Days with a Hart Like a Dog (Hangman Books 1994) for *In Dead Mens Shoes, The Poetry Racket,* & *The Sons of Man* by Billy Childish.

Lust (Gecko Press 1994) for *Playmates* & *Self-Reliance* by Jade Reidy.

Magma (Stukely Press, The City Lit 1994) for *Dali* by Paul Gerhard.

Poetry London Newsletter (PLN Vol. V No. 2, Spring 1994) for *Eating Disorder* by Rosemary Norman.

The Figure in Black (Hearing Eye 1994) for *Father's Rage* by Fatma Durmush.

The Greenman & Skyclad Christ (Laserwolf Books 1994) for *The Greenman* by Bill Lewis.

The Ivy (Aldgate Press 1994) for *Ireland* & *Mike Mosely* by David Kessel.

The Way We Look (Bushy Kelly/Phoenix Appeal 1994) for *Old Age* by Jeanne Wordsworth.

Wordsounds & Sightlines: New & Selected Poems (Sinclair-Stevenson 1994) for *Composed Upon Westminster Bridge 1992* and *Same Old-World-Disorder Blues* by Michael Horovitz.

Mirrorwork (Carcanet 1995) for *Reaching the Midway Mark* by Mimi Khalvati.

And Dream of Mary Magdalen (Clerical Workshop, Maudsley Hospital 1995) for *Comeuppance* and *Little Willie, Down in Peckham?* by Paul Gerhard.

SPECIAL THANKS

SURVIVORS' POETRY gives special thanks to the large number of individuals, groups and organisations who have contributed support and services to its programme and development during the past four years, including:

Patience Agbabi, Kathleen Aitken, Apples & Snakes, John Arthur, The Baffled Angels, Thurstine Basset, Laurence Bayliss, Paul Beasley, Anne Bendall, Peter Beresford, Mandy Berry, Blue Nose Poetry, Anny Brackx, Bradford Coalition of Disabled People, Pauline Bradley, Pauline Bray, Jean Binta Breeze, Chris Brierley, Brixton Community Sanctuary, Bromley Users Group, Martin Brownlee, Brother Niyi, Mary Burguires, Antonia Byatt, Trevor Caits, Campaign Against Psychiatric Oppression, Dave Carter, Dennis Casling, Michael Charles, Chats Palace, City & Hackney *Mind*, Judi Clements, Community Support Network, Terry Cordrey, Anne Curham, Leon Cych, *DAIL* Magazine, Alys Daines, *DAM*, Frank David, Ruby Dawson, *DAN*, Dave Dell, Lynne Dick, Christina Domingo, Jo Doyle, Sonia Dresserkie, Ealing Survivors Forum, Barry Ealy, Eastside Wordcentre, Erconweld Centre, Exeter Survivors' Poetry, Mikey Francis, Ann Franson, Friday Club, John Gash, Lloyd Gee, J. Paul Getty Jr. Charitable Trust, Davy Graham, Greater London Association of Disabled People, Jim Green, Lavinia Greenlaw, Joyoti Gretch, Theresa Griffiths, Roger Grimshaw, Kwabena Gyedu, Julian Harrow, Harwood Road Resettlement Centre, William Hammy Howell, Susan Johns, David Hall, Michael Hambridge, Hampden Community Centre, John Hampson, Wendy Harpe, Merilyn Harris, Ruth Harrison, Angel Hart, Jana Heller, Mandy Holland, Frances Holloway, Joseph Houghey, Brigid Howarth, Roland Humphrey, Graham Jackson, Keith Johnson, Mark Kamara, Ros Kane, David Keay, John Keiffer, Emily Kennedy, Islington Arts & Heritage, Lambeth Advocacy Project, LDAF, Alan Leader, Leeds Survivors Poetry, Gill Levick, Hazel Lewis, Barbara Lisiki, Jackie Lynton, Roy Mackenzie, Ruth Malkin, Manchester Survivors' Poetry, Bol Marjoram, Devon Marston, Colin Mart, Timothy Mason, Iain Matheson, Joe McConnell, Angela McHarron, Gary McKeown, Emma McMullen, Valeria Melchioretto, Sue Melrose, Wendy Metcalf, *Mind* in Camden, *Mind* in Hillingdon, *Mind* in Newham, *Mind* in Richmond & Barnes, *Mind* in Tower Hamlets, Wendy Moore, Quibilah Montsho, Mother Courage, Claire Mooney, Kevin Mulhern, Albert Myers, John Nettle, Alastair Niven, National *Mind*, Nuff Said, Brigid O'Brien Twohig, John O'Neil, Maria Oshodi, Orville Blackwood Campaign, J Owen Williams, Jilly Paver, Amita Patel, Cathy Pelikan, Josa Pepper, Sarath Perera, Andrew Pinnock, Edward Platt, The Poetry Library, Yvonne Poulson, Jean du Pre, Sean Redding, Peter Relton, The Rendezvous, Mark Ross, Sam & Mano Band, Stella Robinson, Peter Rothwell, Antony Rowe, Ructions, Rupa Sarka, Mina Sassoon, Saving Graces, Sarah Scott, *SHAPE* London, Ahmed Sheikh, Yinka Shonibare, Dave Skull, Bill Slade, Alison Smith, Mr Social Control, Neil Sparkes, The Speech Painters, Lizzie Spring, St. Vincents Community Centre, Stockholm Survivors Poetry, Survivors Poetry Merseyside, *Survivors Speak Out*, Roger Symes, Iain Stewart, Ashley Stopforth, Mark Stove, George Tahta, Kath Tait, Steve Tasane, Sean Taylor, Leah Thorn, *Time Out*, The Tiny Teds, Maria Torres, Torriano Poetry, Steve Turner, Sian Vasey, Julie Vasili, Vineyard Project, Katherine Walsh, Dave Ward, Storme Webber, Kit Wells, Julie Williams, Sian Williams, Sue Williams, Jaki Windmill, The Wise Wound, Harold Wolfe, Wolverhampton Survivors' Poetry, Maggie Woolley, World Oyster Club.

. . . . *and to all our friends and associates in every part of the U.K. and throughout the World.*

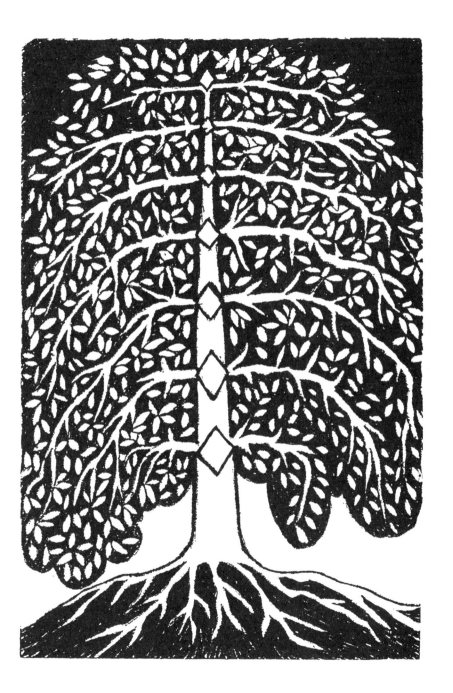